Sweet Theft

SWEET THEFT

A POET'S COMMONPLACE BOOK

J. D. McCLATCHY

COUNTERPOINT

Library of Congress Cataloging-in-Publication Data is available
ISBN 978-1-61902-978-908-8

Design by Chip Kidd

Manuscript images from the collection of the author
Other images curated by Eric Baker

COUNTERPOINT
2560 Ninth Street, Suite 318
Berkeley, CA 94710
www.counterpointpress.com

Printed in the United States of America

For Chip Kidd

who has designed this book
and everything else in my life
for two decades now.

'Tis no sin love's fruit to steal
But the sweet theft to reveal

BEN JONSON

I have from time to time kept both a notebook and a journal. They are very different things, as different as a recipe and the plat du jour. The one book I have scribbled in consistently over the past four decades, though, is my commonplace book, a sort of ledger of envies and joys. "By necessity, by proclivity,—and by delight, we all quote," Emerson observed. I have been drawn to turns of phrase or bits of truth, and the best are combinations of both—as in the work of that sublime revolutionary wit Oscar Wilde. But there is more to it than that. The sentences I hoard are images. And as G. K. Chesterton once wrote: "The original quality in any man of imagination is imagery. It is a thing like the landscape of his dreams; the sort of world he would like to make or in which he would wish to wander; the strange flora and fauna of his own secret planet; the sort of thing he likes to think about." The bower-bird in me is forever collecting colored threads and mirror-shards to make a sort of world. My secret planet is populated by Diana Vreeland and Dwight Eisenhower and Alexander Pope and John Cage and Edgar Degas and Dizzy Gillespie and hundreds of others: a Mad Hatter's tea party of brilliant conversationalists talking over and at odds with one another. I don't use their remarks in my poems; I sometimes quote from them in my prose—and can be seen here gathering possible ways of expressing my scorn or admiration. There is also a recurring character, named X, to whom phrases happen. I have even included some musings of my own, pale by comparison with the wisdom of others but linked by the same impulse. I collect sentences because of the way, in each, something is put that is both precise and surprising. Twice-distilled poems? No. But an abstract model for the poetic. And if a poem is meant to be the light that casts a shadow, many of the entries in this book share the darkness of anyone's skeptical or ironic sensibility. To minimize the risk of tedium, I have assembled here about half of the material I have copied down over the years. Haste and blurry vision may occasionally have introduced some errors into my copying, but if the odd word is off, the sense is there. The range of this book is narrow but high-minded. It limits itself to the sources of art, the relationship of the page to the world, and to aesthetic prowess. But any meditation on art, of course, is a commentary on the life—fetid or fertile, domestic or abstruse, deliberately provocative and endlessly varied— that inspires and sustains it. Proverb or remark, aphorism or anecdote, each gem contains a chaos and functions as a prism, allowing us to contemplate what we didn't know we didn't know.

"Commonplace" means proverbial wisdom. Sages from Cicero to Erasmus kept such books; they were meant to instruct, not to intrigue. Orators and students would study the snippets from moral philosophy and great poems. When books were rare and passed from hand to hand, the keeping of such scrapbooks became a way to preserve favorite passages before having to return the book to its owner. Milton and Leopardi, Emerson and Hardy, E. M. Forster and Alec Guinness kept them. In the eighteenth century, they became more personal and idiosyncratic. What once was considered an educational anthology the dictionary today defines as "a personal journal in which quotable passages, literary excerpts, and comments are written." Emerson made it less a pastime than a noble cause, and gave it a revolutionary American slant: "Make your own Bible. Select and collect all those words and sentences that in all your reading have been to you like the blast of a trumpet out of Shakespeare, Seneca, Moses, John and Paul."

One old term for a commonplace book was silva rerum, "a forest of things." My own favorite is W. H. Auden's alphabetically-arranged A Certain World, published in 1970, a constant wonder of discovery and annotation. Published near the end of his life, it is an emblem of the voracious appetite for knowledge that distinguishes his poems. He found appealing both the sacred and the camp.

This book is meant to be sipped, not gulped. It is not necessarily meant to be read from beginning to end, but to be dipped into, a page or two savored at a time. I hope you wander at will through my forest of things and take from it a part of the pleasure I had in transcribing what the leaves said and the birds sang.

JDMcC

Robert Louis Stevenson: "Sooner or later we all sit down to a banquet of consequences."

A Constant Lambert ditty:
> *It's no good escaping your doom*
> *By taking a ticket to Spain;*
> *The bulging portmanteaux of gloom*
> *Will arrive by a later train.*

There is the story of Poussin impatiently dashing his sponge against his canvas, and producing the precise effect (the foam on a horse's mouth) which he had been long and vainly laboring for.

Swedenborg said Christianity died out on May 5, 1785—when the last spark of truth left its professors.

Théophile Gautier told the Goncourts (*Journals*, March 3, 1862): "The other day Flaubert said to me, 'It's finished. I have only ten more pages to write. But I've already got the ends of the sentences.' You see? He already had the music of the ends of the sentences which he hadn't yet begun."

Thomas Jefferson Hogg, in his *Life of Shelley*, tells of the celebrated mathematician at Cambridge who, at someone's urging, finally read *Paradise Lost*. "I have read your famous poem. I have read it attentively: but what does it prove? There is more instruction in half a page of Euclid! A man might read Milton's poem a hundred, aye, a thousand times, and he would never learn that the angles at the base of an isosceles tri-angle are equal!"

He further mentions "a fussy, foolish little fellow, a banker in a country town," who once said to him: " 'Would you suppose that much of Mr. Wordsworth's poetry was written in the dark; in total darkness. You will hardly credit it, but it is true, perfectly true!' " He went on to explain "that the Lake bard was accustomed to place a pencil and paper by his bedside, and when a bright thought came to him, between the sheets, he wrote down instantly without striking a light, which was a slow process in an age of tinder-boxes, now obsolete, allowing time for fancies less volatile than emanations from the lakes to evaporate; and thus secured it for the benefit of posterity. Through long habit he was able to write correctly and legibly in the dark."

Continuing, Hogg says that "the sagacious little banker added, 'Any man,' said the banker, 'who can write verses in the dark must be a real genuine poet; he must have it in him; there is no use in denying it. Only think! Just consider! There are poems in Mr. Wordsworth's works that I am not by any means sure I could have written myself, either in the daylight, or in the evening, with two wax candles before me; but to have written them in the dark! There can be no mistake about him; we know very well what he is.' "

Hogg related this to Shelley, who experimented with the idea, but "he usually lost his pencil, or his paper, or both; and when he contrived to keep them, the writing was illegible."

—A party: When posh comes to shove.
—den of antiquity

Paul Valéry, from his *Analects*:
   One man is depressed by nightfall.
   Another by the dawn.
   And there is another sadness—of high noon.
   Personally I find the finest day becomes acutely painful toward three in the afternoon. The maturity of its power condemns it; for in it all life lies naked to itself.
   What a queer thing is the Day! Queer in the

sense of alien: foreign to us: foreign to the thinking mind which seems to reason, to create, to define, and to carry on, as the fancy takes it, its orderly or disorderly train of thoughts, with supreme indifference to this vast timepiece of light which measures what it manifests and manifests what it metes out.

But, though unnoticed by the active mind, the stealthy progress of the Day imposes mutations on its forces; that is to say, a varied coloration and relief, a balanced flow of energy, and a diurnal stocktaking of its ideas.

The Day and the Body: two great powers.

An Oscar Wilde bouquet:

He who stands most remote from his age is he who mirrors it best.

It is always with the best intentions that the worst work is done.

Charity creates a multitude of sins.

A thing is not necessarily true because a man dies for it.

What people call insincerity is simply a method by which we can multiply our personalities.

The secret of life is never to have an emotion that is unbecoming.

The highest criticism really is the record of one's own soul. It is more fascinating than history, as it is concerned simply in oneself. It is more delightful than philosophy, as its subject is concrete and not abstract, real and not vague. It is the only civilized form of autobiography, as it deals, not in events, but in the thoughts of one's life, not in life's physical accidents of deed or circumstance, but in the spiritual moods and imaginative passions of the mind.

The object of art is not simple truths but complex beauty.

Everything that is true is inappropriate.

Many a young man starts in life with a natural gift for exaggeration which, if nurtured in congenial and sympathetic surroundings, or by the imitation of the best models, might grow into something really great and wonderful. But, as a rule, he comes to nothing. He either falls into careless habits of accuracy or takes to frequenting the society of the aged and the well-informed. Both things are equally fatal to his imagination.

Lady Henry Wotton was a curious woman, whose dresses always looked as if they had been designed in a rage and put on in a tempest. She was usually in love with somebody, and, as her passion was never returned, she had kept all her illusions. She tried to look picturesque but only succeeded in being untidy.

All art is at once surface and symbol.

An echo is often more beautiful than the voice it repeats.

John Ashbery, as quoted in the Preface to John Bernard Myers' *Poets of the New York School*:
  —Poetry does not have subject matter because it is the subject!
  —The early Auden, Laura Riding, and Wallace Stevens were the writers who most formed my language as a poet.

11.xi.90. In line with Jane for a movie at MOMA. The creepy Samuel Menashe approaches. He said he'd been at my NYU reading last week and been struck by my new Bishop poem. Did I remember the Cambridge reading of long ago? he asked. I did. Did I remember talking with Lowell about Bishop? I didn't. Well, he had been listening in. He overheard me asking Cal what might account for EB's popularity. "All the fags like her" was his answer.

Jung: "He did not think, he perceived his mind functioning."

E. F. Benson on Philip Burne-Jones: "But he lacked the artistic fervor that demands finish for its fulfillment, and perhaps he did not understand that unless there is inspiration in the picture, finish only accentuates the lack of it."

Alexander Pope, letter to Edward Blount (Oct. 3, 1721): " . . . for I see one may go so far as to be Poetical, and hope to save one's Soul at the same time."

Cyril Connolly: "Ennui is the condition of not fulfilling one's potentialities; remorse of not having fulfilled them; anxiety of not being able to fulfill them."

"Deep within me, I know that part of the artist's job is to renew our sense of the comely and the beautiful . . . I have been writing music for forty years. During those years there have been huge and world-shattering events in which I have inevitably been caught up. Whether society has felt music valuable or needful I have gone on writing because I must. And I know that my true function within a society that embraces all of us is to continue an age-old tradition . . . to create images from the depth of the imagination and to give them form . . . Images of the past, shapes of the future. Images of vigor for a decadent period, images of calm for one too violent. Images of reconciliation for worlds torn by division. And, in an age of mediocrity and shattered dreams, images of abounding, generous, exuberant beauty."

—Sir Michael Tippett, "Poets in a Barren Age"

Certain writers are like those ballet dancers who, when bowing, use their elaborate deference to their partners as a means of gathering more applause for themselves.

The difference between baroque music and Beethoven: in the one, form determines; in the other, it defines.

Auden's face: like sweetbreads.

Pound's "make it new" may be an echo of Richard Wagner: "Kinder! Macht Neue! Neue! Und abermals Neues!" [Children! Make it new! New! And again new!]

"An artist paints so that he will have something to look at."
                                        —Barnett Newman

Some poets use the language as if it were a lock which they once picked accidentally—but don't know the combination of.

From Louise Bogan's journal (excerpted in *The New Yorker*): "The unconscious makes its repeated mistakes; it has not seen the reality; it has sensed it merely. The dream Venice is not the Venice experienced; it is all a little wrong. A separate and distinct country is built up, from childhood on, in the dream. It has its cities, its suburbs, its gardens, its hills, and its sea. Other ones. A reflection; a distortion . . . And it repeats its mistakes, as though it had learned them by rote . . . ."

Stendhal: "Le style, c'est ajouter à une pensée donnée toutes les circonstances propres à produire tout l'effet que doit produire cette pensée." [Style consists in supplementing any given thought with all the details necessary for this thought to produce its full effect.]

Flaubert, in a letter: "What seems beautiful to me, what I should most like to do, would be a book about nothing, a book without any exterior ties, but sustained by the internal force of its style . . . a book which would have almost no subject, or at least in which the subject would be almost invisible, if that is possible. The most beautiful works are those with least matter."

"Always be sincere, whether you mean it or not."
　　　　　—Flanders to Swann, "At the Drop of a Hat"

S. J. Perelman is our American Firbank?

Elizabeth Bowen's style—the significant words all sound as if they'd been first crossed-out and replaced, either by a more exact or a more stylized choice.

One publishes his first book to convince himself he is a poet, and publishes his second to convince others.

Elizabeth Bishop's "cold dark deep"—*cold*, not as impersonal or unfeeling, but as exact and unsparing. Chekhov to Gorky: "You must be cold." And is Bishop's "comic" tone primarily Chekhovian?

Blake: "A fool sees not the same tree that a wise man sees."

"What did you do in the War, Mr. Joyce?"
"I wrote *Ulysses*. What did you do?"

"There are worse crimes than burning books. One of them is not reading them."   —Joseph Brodsky

When I first read, on page 34 of the July 17, 1971 issue of *The New Yorker*, Elizabeth Bishop's poem "In the Waiting Room," I was bowled over. It was an extraordinary performance—funny and frightening, casual and profound. One of its strangest sections has the young narrator paging through an office copy of *National Geographic* magazine and seeing extraordinary pictures of an African expedition undertaken by the married adventurers Osa and Martin Johnson. Almost as soon as I read the poem, I went to the Sterling Library at Yale, where I was a graduate student, and searched for the high dusty shelf where I would find the issue Bishop had specified, February, 1918. I found it. There were articles about Alaska, about food shortages for the Allies, about oil shale in Utah. And when, a few weeks later, I ran into Miss Bishop at a party in New York (I remember her telling me how much she hated the new settings of her poems by Elliot Carter), I gushed to her about "In the Waiting Room." Praise seemed to make her face go blank. Then I sheepishly told her of my discovery. She paused for a moment, and said "Oh, it must have been March."

As soon as I returned to New Haven, I rushed to the library stacks. I found the March issue. Why did I not know that the article wouldn't be there either? I had run headlong into my own pedantic literalism, even though it heightened my appreciation of Bishop's powers of "realistic" but composed description. Many years later still, at a flea market, I bought a copy of the February, 1918 issue of the *National Geographic*. To this day, I keep it on my desk, within sight, to remind me of one of the ways I had misread poems over the years.

Art as Fascist—what's the difference between the B-Minor Mass and the Nuremberg rally?

Dante's *Inferno*. Auden quotes someone's remark that the damned don't want to escape. Why? The occurrence of sin has been portrayed as a *condition*, self-contained. This view (say, by medieval man) implies that the sin is in some sense a *pleasure*; so, what's the difference between heaven and hell? If there's a God, there is either a heaven or a hell. The cop-out is to believe in both.

"You only have so many notes, and what makes a style is how you get from one note to another."

—Dizzy Gillespie

Thomas Mann died on my tenth birthday—August 12, 1955—at age eighty-one.

"All things merge into one another—good into evil, generosity into justice, religion into politics…"

—Thomas Hardy

"If language had been the creation, not of poetry, but of logic, we should only have one."   —Hebbel

"Originality does not consist of saying what no one has ever said before, but in saying exactly what you think yourself."   —James Stephens

The Marquis de Sade was descended from the same family as Petrarch's Laura.

"The gods, by right of nature, must possess
An everlasting age of perfect peace;
Far off removed from us and our affairs;
Neither approached by dangers, or by cares;
Rich in themselves, to whom we cannot add;
Nor pleased by good deeds, nor provoked by bad."
—Rochester translation of lines from Lucretius

"Who would be a goody that could be a genius?"
—Margaret Fuller to Emerson,
on the subject of women

Goethe: "In der Beschränkung zeigt sich erst der Meister." (In the limitations the master shows his mastery. That is, literary mastery expresses itself only in the restrictions it accepts. George Kennan is fond of this formulation.)

Henri Cartier-Bresson says he pursues the photographic image in order to record "the beauty of the form; that is, the geometry awakened by what is offered."

"It is something to observe; but it is not enough: we must experiment, that is to say, we must ourselves intervene and create artificial conditions which oblige the animal to reveal to us what it would not tell if left to the normal course of events. . . . Observation sets the problem; experiment solves it, always presuming that it can be solved; or at least, if powerless to yield the full light of truth, it sheds a certain gleam over the edges of the impenetrable cloud."

—Jean-Henri Fabre on the poet's responsibility,
from *The Mason-Wasps*, Chapter 5

—A seat on the last plane out.

For Wallace Stevens, read Saturn's speech at the opening of *Hyperion*.

James Schuyler—sounds halfway between Elizabeth Bishop and John Ashbery. Both of these poets, however "natural" or "distinctive" their style may be described, are very rhetorical. Schuyler prefers "speech" to Style. His is a faux-naïf, Alex Katz approach. He's interested in *meaning*; genial but cautious; scarred.

When I was in college, the study of the *Aeneid* then seemed to stress the prerequisites of duty, the steep cost of both repressed passion and ruthless empire. This was as likely as not an echo of what I was at the same time complaining about to my psychiatrist. Both the poem and my life I saw then as an immense marble staircase with a narrow red runner rising toward an empty sky. Nowadays, at last old enough to read the poem without the burden of either being deaf to its emotional appeal or of having to carry it on my shoulders from some burning classroom, it seems an altogether different work, at once smaller in scope and larger in resonance. Two strains have come to dominate. First, I watch it all—voyage or contest or battle, camp or palace—through a scrim, the *sfumato* effect of sadness. The sadness is neither grief nor weariness. It is psychological perspective and moral tone. Virgil wrote the consummate elegy of aftermath. Second—and in this he resembles no writer more than Proust—the *Aeneid* is a poem about memory, its intolerable system of weights and releases, the screech owl beating against the shield. Memory is fury and muse, and drives the poem's plot and characters. The poet's use of prophecy—"hindsight as foresight" in Auden's scolding phrase—is his shuttle. No earlier poem, and few later, pleated time so seamlessly. The past can force a civilization, or turn a heart inside out. In either case, only suffering is finally of use. Like his master Lucretius, Virgil saw love and war—Venus the

mother of Aeneas, and Mars the father of Romulus—
as the ancestors of Rome, as they are of memory itself, which both restores and festers. Just so is peace,
whether in the lonely hearts of all the poem's heroes
or in the realm of the Pax Augusta, an aftermath dis-
tilled from sadness and memory, if only sadness en-
shrined and memories projected. And the style of it
all? On the swags of syntactical and narrative brocade,
the emotional pattern is stitched with a simple and
subtle clarity. The half-light against which the poet's
images flicker the more briefly and brilliantly dims
until Dante and seems, after Leopardi and Montale,
to be characteristically Italian. English's more gar-
ish and insistent maneuvers miss the cloudy linings
of silvered words—though Robert Fitzgerald captures
more than any translator has, or probably could. The
poem's symphonic organization, its harmonies and
modulations, its swelling set-pieces and tender ges-
tures, together define the lyrical epic. Pallas on his
pyre, his head wrapped in Dido's gold-woven cloth,
the trophies of war piled over the naked youth, and
Aeneas's tight-lipped farewell . . . it is at such passages that the lines blur. Rarely has a public moment
been rendered so intimately, or the private life so elo-
quently modeled into monumental sculpture.

When asked as a child what he wanted to be when
he grew up, the great Austrian stage designer Alfred
Roller said: "someone who is allowed to go backstage."

"Great art consists of showing, through faultless self-possession, that we are on the heights of ecstasy, without revealing how we reached them."
—Mallarmé, letter to Henri Cazalis, April 25, 1864

SM—Describes not the object itself, but the effect it produces.

A verse: not words, but intentions.

"Scale" means both proportion and tonality.

Gothic arches—as crisp and chaste as whimples.

As a requiem (music) or an elegy (poetry), the occasion and motive are still a force and presence. There's always a corpse. In a Mass, say the B-minor, there is no necessary sense of a mass in progress.

John Keats to Richard Woodhouse, October 27, 1818 letter: "What shocks the virtuous philosopher, delights the chameleon poet. [Poetry] does no harm from its relish of the dark side of things, any more than from its taste for the bright one—because they both end in speculation." (Notice the *dark* relish and the bright *taste*.)

The moralist takes true and false to be right and wrong.

A contemporary reviewer found "The Ancient Mariner" a "rhapsody of unintelligible wildness and incoherence."

Pope, in the *Art of Sinking*, describes the way of "obliquely waddling to the mark in view." (periphrasis)

John Webster: "Like diamonds we are cut with our own dust."

Looking back at the end of his life on his diplomatic service—flipflopping from royalist to revolutionary and back to royalist—Prince Tallyrand is reputed to have said: "You can do many things with bayonets, but it is rather uncomfortable to sit on them."

Plato, *Laws*: "The beginning is like a god, who while he lives among men redeems all."

—like a dog, whose text is territory, and he puts his yellow High-Lighter over its significances.

X's style of poems: a sugar pill with a bitter coating.

—cheap frills
—splice of life

"A history only of departed things / Or a mere fiction of what never was?"   —William Wordsworth,
The Recluse (1888), ll. 803-804

John Ashbery, speaking of the nouveaux roman-istes' debt to Raymond Roussel, mentions functional tedium.

Saint-Saens—arrangements of Wagner played by a café orchestra.

The modern popularity of the harpsichord is a product of technological futurism—the *sound* of metal.

A way to judge poetry anthologies: don't look first to the poets included; look to the kind of poems the anthologist chooses to represent any one of (and all) the poets. Is there a point or program?

Once when he was asked, "Why do you write?" Paul Valéry answered, "Through weakness" (Par faiblesse).

John Ashbery, referring to his and Frank O'Hara's undergraduate poetry, has said it "now seems marred by a certain nervous preciosity, in part a reaction to the cultivated blandness around us which also impelled us to callow aesthetic pronouncements." So too with *Some Trees* and *The Tennis Court Oath*—they seem written in reaction, rather than in response, to ancestral or personal voices.

Listening to Billie Holiday sing Cole Porter: whose song is it?

Maria Callas: "Opera is the most noble and beautiful way of speaking."

"Some writers confuse authenticity, which they ought always to aim at, with originality, which they should never bother about."   —W. H. Auden

Oscar Hammerstein's formula for the book of a musical: The first act should be twice as long as the second, and twice as much should happen in the second than in the first.

Mary Martin suffered from stage fright, and once told how she dealt with it: "It's very simple. I come to the theater half an hour before the half-hour call, and get made up, and get into my costume. When they call the half hour I go into the john and I stay there until Gladys [the maid] comes and says, 'You're on, Miss Martin.' Then I lean down, pull up my panties, and go out on-stage. Well, that's the way you deal with stage fright."

"Give us this day our daily idea and forgive us all we thought yesterday."   —Bernard Berenson

"The philosopher may sometimes love the infinite; the poet always loves the finite. For [the poet] the great moment is not the creation of light, but the creation of the sun and the moon."   —G. K. Chesterton

"Bitter and gay, that is the heroic mood."
                                        —Ernest Dowson

Oscar Wilde: "What the paradox was to me in the sphere of thought, perversity became to me in the sphere of passion."—"For a sentimentalist is simply one who desires to have the luxury of an emotion without paying for it."

Speaking of Auden, Richard Howard says "Heavy Date" and "Lullaby" ("Lay your sleeping head") are early closeted poems; "Since" and "The Common Life" are late, more open.

Four Auden limericks:

>The Bishop Elect of Hong Kong
>Had a dong that was twelve inches long.
>He thought the spectators
>Were admiring his gaiters
>When he went to the gents. He was wrong.

>There is an old queen we call Sims,
>Who always hums when she rims.
>An unusual ass
>Gets the B-minor Mass,
>But the rest all get Anglican hymns.

>A man came out of the mists.
>He had the most beautiful wrists.
>Some scandals occurred
>Which have long been interred,
>But the legend about him persists.

>As the poets have mournfully sung,
>Death comes to the innocent young.
>The rolling in money,
>The screamingly funny,
>And those who are very well hung.

Auden palindrome: T. Eliot, topbard, notes putrid tang emanating is sad. I'd assign it a name: gnat dirt upset on drab pot toilet.

James Merrill limerick:

> There was a young lady named Linda
> Who used to undress by the window.
> Her left hand would lust
> Over belly and bust,
> While the right turned the page of Pindar.

How I Met James Merrill

In the early 70s, I had been reading his poems in *The New Yorker*, and when they were gathered in *Braving the Elements*—a book that mesmerized me—I wrote a fan letter to the poet in care of his publisher. Some months later, a blue air-letter arrived from Greece. It was the poet, with his charming thanks. I had meanwhile purchased at an old bookstore the diary of a young 19th-century American woman on her first trip abroad. It included her account of having attended the premiere of *La Traviata*. She had no idea what she had heard but was fascinated by the fact that the next day everyone in the streets was singing its tunes. I sent the diary to JM, and he responded with delight. That started a correspondence, and eventually he suggested I come to a reading he would be giving in a few months with Elizabeth Bishop at the 92nd Street YMHA in New York. I did. Miss Bishop read first and when she was done she slipped back into the audience to listen to JM, the best reader of poetry there ever was. When he had finished and gone backstage, Miss Bishop lingered in the first row. Manners told me to go up to her and thank her, but when I did she peremptorily told me to fetch her watch which she had accidentally left on the lectern. I went on stage, found her watch, and returned it to her. (She took it without thanking me.) So, by the time I reached the reception, the public had surrounded JM, and every time he reached for a cigarette and tried to light it, another reader would ask for his autograph. The next time he tried, I took my lighter, reached through three rings of people, and held it to his cigarette. He lit up, in both senses. I said, "I'm Sandy McClatchy." He looked up and exclaimed, "So *you're* Sandy McClatchy!" When we finally got to speak, he suggested I come for dinner some night in Stonington. I readily agreed, and a few days later he sent me a postcard with driving directions to his home. I remember how he said I would recognize it. It used to be painted "a dull aubergine but is now a shade of leg makeup." I couldn't miss it.

Love's Labours Lost, Berowne, I, i 141:
> So study evermore is overshot.
> While it doth study to have what it would,
> It doth forget to do the things it should
> And when it have the things it hunteth most,
> 'Tis won as towns with fire—so won, so lost.

Berowne, I, i, 274
> This is not so well as I looked for, but the best that ever I heard.

Robert Browning—"Plain, plump fact"

"Into the mind sensitive to 'form', a flood of random
sounds, colours, incidents, is ever penetrating from
the world without, to become, by sympathetic selec-
tion, a part of its very structure, and, in turn, the visible vesture and expression of that other world it sees
so steadily within, nay, already in a partial conformity
thereto, to be refined, enlarged, corrected, at a hundred points."   —Walter Pater

William Shakespeare, Sonnet 106
    For we, which now behold these present days,
    Have eyes to wonder, but lack tongues to praise.

Love's Labours Lost, Holofernes: "Here are only numbers ratified" . . . "the jerks of invention"

Love's Labours Lost, Berowne, a gay passage: IV, iii, 213:
    Sweet lords, sweet lovers, O let us embrace!
    As true we are as flesh & blood can be.
    The sea will ebb and flow, heaven show his face;
    Young blood doth not obey an old decree.

We cannot cross the cause why we were born;
Therefore of all hands must we be forsworn.

Love's Labours Lost, Moth: "They have been at a great feast of languages, and stol'n the scraps."

Gerard Manley Hopkins—Swinburne with spondees.

Three types of people in society: the good enough, the better-off, and the best by far.

—A drab moth that attracts so many bright flames.

Jacques Lacan: "The function of language is not to inform but to evoke."

Certain writers:
    1. like walking the net without a tightrope.
    2. a voyeur, but one who prefers spying through frosted glass.

—If it moves, salute it; if it doesn't, polish it.
—All that's gold doesn't glitter.
—X has a glittering —. But all is not gold.

"Do not, reader, suspect that because I am choosing my words nicely, and playing with metaphor, and putting my commas in their proper places, my sorrow is not really and truly poignant. I write elaborately, for that is my habit, and habits are less easily broken than hearts."   —Max Beerbohm

Our reactions (by which we're apprehended and judged) are much more limited than our comprehension of things (unlanguaged), which is often more than we have words for or command of.

Henry David Thoreau, from "Friendship":
"I have never known one who could bear criticism, who could not be flattered, who would not bribe his judge, or was content that the truth should be loved always better than himself."

Virginia Woolf, *Diary*, II, 253:
"I don't object to opening the heart, but I do object to finding it empty."

Van Gogh, in an 1885 letter to the Dutch artist Anthon van Rappard: "I am always doing *what I can't do yet* in order to learn how to do it."

Yes, scientific theories become the poet's metaphors. But theories themselves may be as dependent on available metaphors (i.e., phenomenon having become image) as on technology. Newton, with his gravity and apple, had read Milton. Einstein, with his relativity and space-time, had read Goethe's *Faust*. Even so, Albert Einstein's theory of relativity, say, depended on trains and elevators: not just new perspectives, but also enabling images.

Lu Ki, *Wan Fu*: the five qualities of good writing: music, harmony, sadness, decorum, richness.

Djuna Barnes, *Nightwood*: "An image is a stop the mind makes between uncertainties."

Sachlichkeit — a prosy, matter-of-fact manner of putting things.

Howard Moss: "The truest changes in art are not changes of technique but of sensibility. And so the real pioneers are rarely recognized as such. They are too subtle to make good copy. Examples: Henry Green and Elizabeth Bishop."

Translation. If one reads French, he should read Italian or Spanish or Russian poetry in French translation rather than English. It preserves the sense of estrangement; and one is not thereby distracted by the arbitrary importance of both the original language and English.

defiant — deviant

Marianne Moore, speaking of her poem "Marriage": "It's just an anthology of words that I didn't want to lose, that I liked very much, and I put them together as plausibly as I could. So people daren't derive a whole philosophy of life from *that*."

William Hazlitt: "If a person has no delicacy, he has you in his power."

∞

Peter DeVries imagined a boîte for elderly merrymakers called the Slipped Discotheque.

∞

Madame du Deffand, on reading the Bible: "Quel ton! Quel effroyable ton!" [What a style! What a dreadful style!]

∞

Item from a small English county newspaper:
"In the unlikely event of seeing a garden warbler, it may be recognized by the absence of any distinguishing feature."

∞

Heine on his deathbed, refusing a priest: "Dieu me pardonnera, c'est son métier." [God will pardon me. That's his business.]

∞

Léon Rivas, the priest-turned-revolutionary in Graham Greene's 1973 novel, *The Honorary Consul*, explaining his belief in God: "The God I believe in must be responsible for all the evil as well as for all the saints. He has to be a God made in our image with a night-side as well as a day-side. When you speak of the horror, Eduardo, you are speaking of the night-side of God. I believe the time will come when the night-side will wither away, like your communist state, Aquino, and we shall see only the simple day-light of the good God. You believe in evolution, Eduardo, even though sometimes whole generations of men slip backwards to the beasts. It is a long suffering, evolution, and I believe God is suffering the same evolution as we are, but perhaps with more pain."

— I feel like Jesus kissing Judas.
— All chip and no shoulder
— X has a gumdrop for a brain
— the *Lumpenstudenten*

Bits from *The Wings of the Dove*:

Preface:

      — "the interesting state"

      — "inspired resistance"

      — Americans are "heirs of all the ages"

      — the appearances of Venice are "rich and obscure and portentous"

— Merton Densher represents to Kate Croy "all the high dim things she lumped together as of the mind."

— "Mrs. Lowder, it was true, steering in the other quarter a course in which she called on subjects as if they were islets in an archipelago."

— Susie had an instant thought and then an effusion.
"My dear child, we move in a labyrinth."
"Of course we do. That's just the fun of it!" said Milly with a strange gaiety. Then she added: "Don't tell me that—in this for instance—there are not abysses. I want abysses."

— He faced it all, and certainly it was queer. But it wasn't the queerness that after another minute was uppermost. He was in a wondrous silken web, and it was amusing. "You spoil me!"

— "Awful?" A sound of impatience—the form of a laugh—at last escaped her. "I can't find it anything at all till I know what you're talking about."

Sir Francis Bacon refers to a "cobweb-lawn," "so tender that it feels everything."

"He used to be a great artist, but now he's only a genius."   —Braque on Picasso

Andrew Lloyd Weber is reported to have once asked Alan Jay Lerner: "Why do people take an instant dislike to me?" Lerner replied: "It saves time."

"My writing is scarcely for the public ear. I have no luck traveling. I'm ashamed to accept payment for reading. I resent people who won't buy your books coming to gawk at a writer. All the readings I've done were to oblige friends whose feelings I didn't want to hurt by refusing."—Guy Davenport, from an interview

Of his wife Camille on her deathbed Monet writes: "I found myself, without being able to help it, in a study of my beloved wife's face, systematically noting the colors."

"I know the wages of Pleasure, the sweet strain,
The lullings and the relishes of it."
                              —George Herbert, "The Pearle"

"A comedy that ends with marriage is the beginning of a tragedy."   —Sacha Guitry

Stendhal, from *De L'Amour*:
　　— The thing is that they [women] are hungry for emotion, anywhere and at any time: think of the pleasures of a Scottish funeral.
　　— I am continually hurt by the fear that I may have expressed only a sigh when I thought I was stating a truth.

In Europe desire is whetted by constraint; in America it is blunted by liberty.

Ford Madox Ford, *Provence*:
"I must confess that I find all poets difficult to talk to. A poet speaking to a mere *proseteur* has always—and no doubt rightly—the air of a Bourbon Prince talking to an Orleanist Sovereign, as if we had usurped the land that he should have inherited. Yes, no doubt rightly. Prose is infinitely more difficult to write and vastly the more agreeable to read but it does not confer any divine right upon its advocates."

". . . l'idée fixe produit les miracles des évasions et les miracles du sentiment . . ."

[...obsessions result in miraculous escapes and miraculous feelings...]   —Balzac, *Le Cousin Pons*

"Write when you find sex."

Ford Madox Ford says Joseph Conrad said: "Le bien l'ennemi du mieux." Ford translates: "The pretty good is the enemy of what is best."

Henry James, *The Golden Bowl* preface:

p. 8: . . . the muffled majesty of authorship.

p. 9: . . . absolutely no refinement of ingenuity or of precaution need be dreamed of or wasted in that most exquisite of all good causes the appeal to variety, the appeal to incalculability, the appeal to a high refinement and a handsome wholeness of effect.

George Barker, from "Asterisks" (1964):

I think that one of the laws of Poetry may be a sort of

hysterical perversity: that is, the poem has a natural hatred of existing, and therefore needs to escape the condition of capture. It dodges, and in dodging, hides behind trees and bushes and street corners which turn out, in the end, to be the poem itself.

The kingdoms of the heart suffer too many palace revolutions. Their dynasties are never secure: obscure heroes and heroines are always about to seize the throne of blood.

Justice is what happens to other people.

So, in the end, Hemingway showed he was a really good shot.

Ahab feels defeated because he knows that Moby is not obsessed by him.

The mind of Ezra Pound looks like a china shop after the bull's visit.

The heart is haunted by the idea that it can do no right and the head by the idea that it can do no wrong.

The conversation of lovers in bed is an elegy disguised as an eclogue.

—a critic named Dr. Malatesta
—a reader named Farfan

"One only writes well about things one hasn't experienced."   —Remy de Gourmont

J'embrasse mon rival mais c'est pour l'étouffer. [I embrace my rival but only to suffocate him.]

Since X exists, we do not have to invent him!

1915, Alfred Stieglitz about Georgia O'Keeffe: "Finally a woman on paper."

X's imagination works at short range.

X writes with her toes turned out, uses the French when she can't think of the English for a thing, and remembers who she is.

—run a mousetrap through her hair and squirt on a little eau de quelquechose

"Blaming a critic is like blaming the rain."
                                        —Vladimir Nabokov

QUATRAIN—sounds like a brand of medicine.

Marianne Moore:
    —"Ecstasy affords / the occasion and expediency determines the form."

    —"What I write, as I have said before, could only be called poetry because there is no other category in which to put it."

"In each art the difficulty of the form is a substitution for the difficulty of direct apprehension and expression of the object. The first difficulty may be more or less overcome, but the second is insuperable; thus every poem begins, or ought to, by a disorderly retreat to defensible positions. Or, rather, by a perception of the hopelessness of direct combat, and a resort to the warfare of spells, effigies, and prophecies. The relation between the artist and reality is an oblique one, and indeed there is no good art which is not consciously oblique. If you respect the reality of the world, you know that you can approach that reality only by indirect means."   —Richard Wilbur

"Straight is the line of Duty;
Curved is the line of Beauty;
Follow the straight line, thou shalt see
The curved line ever follow thee."

> —William McCall, 19th century

With X, one wants more disarray in the dress [or vice versa].

X is fading into notoriety.

"A photograph is a mirror with a memory."

> —Robert de Montesquiou

George Painter's *Proust*:

II, p. 307:

"Style, Proust maintains, must be renewed in each writer, since it consists not in adhesion to a classic model, but in the moment of identification between the author and his subject."

II, p. 306:

"It is the oldest trick in that parasitic trade [of book reviewing] to blame an author for writing about the subject of his book."

II, p. 125:

"Saint-Beuve maintained that the supreme test of critical insight lay in the ability to detect genius among one's contemporaries; yet he consistently underrated the truly original writers of his own time, such as Stendhal, Balzac, Baudelaire and Flaubert."

The Taming of the Shrew:
I, i, 50: "I found the effect of love in idleness." (Lucentio)
I, ii, 250: "Sir, give him head: I know he'll prove a jade." (Lucentio)
IV, i, 120: "And Gabriel's pumps were all unpink'd i' the heel." (Grumio)

Walt Whitman, *Democratic Vistas* (1871):
" . . . sort of male odalisque, singing or piano-playing a kind of spiced ideas, second-hand reminiscences, or toying late hours at entertainments in rooms stifling with fashionable scent."

Whitman described the "so-called literature" of his time as an "endless supply of small coin."

431 Stevens St.
Camden N Jersey
May 22 '76

I Know the bearer Walter
H Ortlip — have known him for
two years. He has work'd here in
this city in a weekly newspaper
office. He is intelligent well
behaved — & for his age, (18) a
very fair Compositor — can set
6 to 7000 ems a day — He lives
in Camden with his parents,
(who are friends of mine.) I un-
hesitatingly recommend him to
any printing office wanting a
young man.

Walt Whitman

Peintre, fuis l'aquarelle,
Et fixe la couleur
Trop frêle
Au four de l'emailleur.
[Painter, avoid watercolors
And let colors too frail
Harden
In the enameller's oven.]   —Gautier, "L'Art" (1857)

Elizabeth Bishop—her poetry *filtered*—her inner voice heard by a hundred objections ("too sentimental," "too cold," "unlikely!," "did that really ever happen to you," "haven't you used that adjective before?," "does it scan?")

John Ashbery—it's hard to read, the way the future is.

A clay idol, with feet of gold / golden feet

Mr. Hodge [the first Philistine] & Mr. Hazard [the last Romantic poet]

Igor Stravinsky: "Inspiration is like a baby: you have to sit it on the pot every morning."

Samuel Johnson: "Nothing is more hopeless than a scheme of merriment."

Johnson on James Macpherson's Ossian: "A man might write such stuff for ever, if he *would* abandon his mind to it."

Johnson on Milton's *Paradise Lost*: "None ever wished it longer than it is."

There is a typological similarity between Satan leaving Eden and Eros leaving Psyche's bed.

The 20th century's characteristic innovations: collage and abstraction.

"Conventions do not arise without some reason, and genius will know how to rise above them by a fresh appreciation of their rightness, and will feel no temptation to overturn them in favour of personal whimsies."   —George Santayana,
"The Elements and Functions of Poetry,"
Interpretations of Poetry and Religion (1900)

Much Ado About Nothing, II, 3, Benedict on Claudio-in-love: " . . . but now is he turn'd orthography, his words are a very fantastical banquet, just so many strange dishes."

Ralph Waldo Emerson, *Journal*, March 20, 1842:
"I do not like the *Plain Speaker* so well as the *Edinburgh Review*. The spirit of the last may be conventional and artificial, but that of the first is coarse, sour, indigent, dwells in a cellar kitchen, and goes to make suicides."

W. H. Auden: "Technique in itself cannot make a good poem, but the lack of it can spoil one."

This book will be read when every other volume of poetry published this year has been long forgotten. But not until then.

Concord
April 10, 1874

Messrs Welch, Bigelow, & Co.

Gentlemen, Please
permit Messrs J. R. Osgood
& Company to print 150 copies
from the Plates of
"Representative Men."

& oblige yours respectfully,

R. W. Emerson

—Spray of stars
—Stew of stars (?)
— leave no turn of phrase unstoned
— let lying dogs sleep
— of a cheapness only money could buy
— read between the lines on his face / brow

"Just play the text, not what it reminds you of."
—Arthur Miller

My poems are often about my own body—the one thing I am certain I know best. It is little wonder that most of us, on waking each morning, can't remember our dreams. Dreams are often so strange, so frightening, so epic and transformational, much more so than anything in our waking lives. But why do we so easily forget them? I think the reason is that dreams are notional, not physical. What we know of pleasure and pain, of embarrassment and pride, we know in or on our bodies. Scar or hicky or cyst, arousal or arthritis, hangover or heartbreak, the body is our ledger.

"Our Western ballet is a clear if complex blending of human anatomy, solid geometry and acrobatics offered as a symbolic demonstration of manners—the

morality of consideration for one human being moving in time with another." —Lincoln Kirstein,
"What Ballet Is All About"

"Look here, Miró, at your age, making paintings like this!" —Picasso to Miró (as reported by Balthus)

Diana Trilling, on herself as a critic, would tell the story of a Viennese novelist, a refugee from Nazi Austria who "was said to have remarked that he had lost his country, his home, his language, but that he had at least one good fortune; he has not been reviewed by me."

"You must come again when you have less time."
—Walter Sickert, showing Denton Welch to the door

As You Like It, III,ii, 175: Rosalind: "I was never so berhymed since Pythagoras' time that I was an Irish rat, which I can hardly remember."

Proust, *Contre Sainte-Beuve et Essais* (Pleiade edition):
p. 382: La vraie beauté est en effet la seule chose qui ne puisse répondre à l'attente d'une imagination

chose. Je ne veux pas promettre ce que je ne
suis pas absolument certain de pouvoir tenir,
d'quoi un moment pourrait - il être certain
d'une chose pourtant, et de cette sympa-
thie dont il vous prie de trouver ici l'expression la plus distinguée Marcel Proust

Monsieur,

Je viens d'être mourant
et c'est bien la seule excuse
— très vraie, très bonne, très

mauvaise — pour mon

retard à vous répondre. Votre

lettre m'a plu infiniment. Je

serai très flatté que vous m'ins-

crivez parmi vos collaborateurs. Quant

à ma collaboration, c'est hélas autre

romanesque. [True beauty is, indeed, the one thing that cannot meet the expectations of a romantic imagination.]

p. 384: à travers un vitrail ou une rampe.
[through stained glass or a flight of stairs]

p. 418: Le poète éprouve et fait connaître avec allégresse la beauté de toutes choses, d'un verre d'eau aussi bien que des diamants, mais aussi des diamants aussi bien que du verre d'eau, d'un champ aussi bien que d'une statue, mais d'une statue aussi bien que d'un champ. [The poet experiences and enthusiastically transmits the beauty of all things, be it a glass of water or diamonds, but diamonds as well a glass of water; be it a field or a statue, but a statue as well as a field.]

p. 303: la chanson sans tons. [toneless song]

p. 665: on Watteau as first painter of modern love: "un sorte d'impuissance ornée." [a kind of adorned impotence]

p. 649: . . . chacun de nous étant asservi aux faits par lesquels l'esprit de vérité et d'inspiration se communiqué à lui [...everyone of us being subservient to the facts through which truth and inspiration are spiritually communicated to us]

p. 650: l'inspiration, le moment où l'esprit prend contact avec soi-même, où la parole intérieure n'a plus rien de la conversation et nie l'homme en tant qu'être causeur et discuteur [inspiration, the moment when the mind is in contact with itself, when the inner word no longer has anything in common with conversation, nullifying man as a talkative, argumentative creature]

p. 651: la culture est comme les bonnes manières de l'esprit [culture is a kind of politeness of the mind]

Debussy about Wagner: "a sunset mistaken for a sunrise."

—*cloisonnisme*

Age is a caricature of the self (or the self's body and features). To make someone look "funny," make him look older.

"I am an artist; consequently, not a liberal."
                                        —Alexander Blok, 1918

"All great poets naturally and fatally become critics."   —Baudelaire,
        "Richard Wagner et Tannhauser à Paris" (1861)

Henry IV, Part I:
    I, iii, 207, Worcester: "He apprehends a world

of figures here / But not the form of what he should attend."

II, ii, 45, Falstaff:
"And I / have not ballads made on you all and sung to filthy / tunes, let a cup of sack be my poison"

III, I, 130, Hotspur:
"I had rather hear a brazen canstick turned,
Or a dry wheel grate on the axle tree,
And that would set my teeth nothing on edge,
Nothing so much as mincing poetry"

∞

"Nobody ever went broke underestimating the taste of the American public."   — H. L. Mencken

∞

The Tempest, II, i, 15, Sebastian's aside to Antonio about Gonzalo: "Look, he's winding up the watch of his wit; by and by it will strike."

∞

After a visit to Ringling Brothers: how America itself is like a three-ring circus—bigger and better, the distracting, exhilarating dazzle, the constant motion, feats and glitter, the ringmaster's hyperbole, and the real daring: a clown on stilts and a somersaulting trapeze artist are momentarily at the same height.

"If it ain't a pleasure, it ain't a poem."

       —William Carlos Williams

"When a true genius appears in the world, you may know him by this sign, that the dunces are all in confederacy against him."   —Jonathan Swift

"The business of America is business."

        —Calvin Coolidge

"Whenever my view strikes them [my critics] as being at all outside the range of, say, an ordinary suburban churchwarden, they conclude that I am echoing Schopenhauer, Nietzsche, Ibsen, Strindberg, Tolstoy, or some other heresiarch in northern or eastern Europe."

 —George Bernard Shaw, preface to *Major Barbara*

Diaghilev and Misia Sert agreed that high art had had its day. They referred to the works of their new friends as "les petites crottes adorables" [adorable little turds].

James Russell Lowell on Edgar Allan Poe, in *A Fable for Critics*, 1848: "Three-fifths of him genius and two-fifths sheer fudge."

Modernisn's concern for "the mind of Europe." T. S. Eliot, Ezra Pound > Czeslaw Milosz, Joseph Brodsky. Contemporary poetry has largely abandoned that.

C'est le premier pas qui coûte. [It's the first step that counts.]

ouvrage de commande [commissioned work]

Valéry says that the real subject of "La Jeune Parque" is "the depiction of a succession of psychological substitutions."

Concerning paraphrases of poems in criticism—any scientific formula (e.g., $E=mc^2$)—is a paraphrase too.

"Poetry is nothing but literature reduced to the essential of its active principle. It has been purged of idols of all kinds, of illusions of realism and of the possible confusion between the language of 'truth' and the language of 'creation.'"   —Paul Valéry

"If poetry has to include silliness, if it can be measured according to the capacity of inferior minds, if Musset is enough to satisfy you, if poetry is allowed to use crude methods, if a mosaic of images is a poem, then to hell with poetry."   —Paul Valéry

Picasso to Gertrude Stein: "Ah, James Joyce—an obscure writer whom all the world can understand."

W. B. Yeats: "A good writer should be so simple that he has no faults, only sins."

Debussy called Fauré *maître des charmes*.

Car nous voulons la Nuance encor
Pas la Couleur, rien que la nuance!

[For we also want Nuance,
No color, only Nuance!]

> —Paul Verlaine, "Art poetique" (1885)

"Great men die twice, once as men, once as great men."

> —Paul Valéry

Valéry felt that most poetry was niaiserie et sottise [silliness and stupidity].

The world of Poetry Workshops — universal suffrage!

X belongs to the Third World of poetry—undernourished, overpopulated, etc.

"The diffusion of taste is not the same thing as the improvement of taste; but it is only the former of these objects that is promoted by public institutions and other artificial means. The number of candidates for fame, and of pretenders to criticism, is thus increased beyond all proportion, while the quantity of genius and feeling remains the same; with this difference, that the man of genius is lost in the crowd of competitors, who would never have become such but from encouragement and example; and that the opinion of those few persons whom nature intended for judges, is drowned in the noisy suffrages of shallow smatterers in taste.

"The principle of universal suffrage, however applicable to matters of government, which concern the common feelings and common interests of society, is by no means applicable to matters of taste, which can only be decided upon by the most refined understandings. The highest efforts of genius, in every walk of art, can never be properly understood by the generality of mankind: There are numberless beauties and truths which lie far beyond their comprehension. It is only as refinement and sublimity are blended with other qualities of a more obvious and grosser nature, that they pass current with the world. Taste is the highest degree of sensibility, or the impression made on the most cultivated and sensible minds, as genius is the result of the highest powers both of feeling and invention. It may be objected, that the public taste is capable of gradual improvement, because, in the end, the public do justice to works of the greatest merit. This is a mistake. The reputation ultimately, and often slowly affixed to works of genius, is stamped upon them by authority, not by popular consent or the common sense of the world. We imagine that the admiration of the works of celebrated men has become common, because the admiration of their names has become so. But does not every ignorant connoisseur pretend the same veneration, and talk with the same vapid assurance

of Michael Angelo, though he has never seen even a copy of any of his pictures, as if he had studied them accurately,—merely because Sir Joshua Reynolds has praised him? Is Milton more popular now than when the *Paradise Lost* was first published? Or does he not rather owe his reputation to the judgment of a few persons in every successive period, accumulating in favour, and overpowering by its weight the public indifference? Why is Shakespeare popular? Not from his refinement of character or sentiment, so much as from his powerful telling of a story,—the variety and invention,—the tragic catastrophe and broad farce of his plays? Spenser is not yet understood. Does not Boccaccio pass to this day for a writer of ribaldry, because his jests and lascivious tales were all that caught the vulgar ear, while the story of the Falcon is forgotten!"   —William Hazlitt,
        from "Why the Arts Are Not Progressive" (1814)

Deconstruction — the nouvelle cuisine of criticism.

In *Twelfth Night*, "the trick of singularity" and the fool is so identified because he is a "corruptor of words."

X is Central Casting's idea of Y.

it loin d'être brillante, mais je
cepter, à condition, bien entendu, que
prises en considération. Il faudrait
puisse voir chaque page, et puis les
lusieurs grosses bevues. Vous les
copie que je vous renvoie.

tre une personne intelligente, mais
en temps son anglais cloche.

t raison: je n'attache pas beaucoup
livres soient publiés en France
ce que, dans mon for interieur, je ne
saurait manquer de venir quand ils y
t pourtant être ingrat que d'annuler,
de tous les efforts que vous avez bien
publiés.

à mes sentiments de sincère amitié.

Vladimir Nabokov

et-vient de lettres et documents, je cro
ciser ce qui suit:
que dans le contrat il ne saurait être
e publication en volume de la traductio
oits (film etc.) me resteraient réserve
ent à effectuer ici et en dollars.
t être exacte et complète, sans changem

Arnold Schoenberg said the only way to appreciate a building is by studying the blueprint.

For someone with a poetic prose style > cf. Mallarmé, "The Crisis in Verse": "There is verse as soon as diction is emphatic, rhythm as soon as there is style."

At a rehearsal of Tchaikovsky's "Pathètique" Symphony, Sir Thomas Beecham began by addressing the orchestra: "Alright, gentlemen, let's see what we can do to cheer it up."

"The world is a kind of delicate meeting place between imagination and knowledge. There is a point, arrived at by diminishing large things and enlarging small ones, that is intrinsically artistic."
—Vladimir Nabokov

Poems aspire, not to the condition of music, but to the status of scripture. (cf. Zohar)

Asked what he thought of his critics, Eugene O'Neill replied, "I love every bone in their heads."

ᴖ

"Brush it! Brush it! Make it absolutely glisten, darling."   —Diana Vreeland

ᴖ

When I was in high school, my literary hero was Vladimir Nabokov, and every year for his April 22nd birthday I would send a congratulatory card to him at his Montreux hotel. Needless to say, there was never a response. But decades later, while doing research at the Berg Collection in the New York Public Library, I was startled when a sub-librarian tapped my shoulder and asked me to accompany him into the vaults. On a table was a numbered box from the Nabokov archive, which the Library has purchased from the writer's family. He told me to open it. There were all my birthday cards.

ᴖ

As *boredom* is an anagram of *bedroom*, so *hater* is an anagram of *heart*.

ᴖ

"The utmost ambition is to lodge a few poems where they will be hard to get rid of."   —Robert Frost

"Art is limitation; the essence of every picture is the frame."
                                        —G. K. Chesterton

"Few will dare or deign to dispute that the prime object of composing poetry is to keep any two poems from sounding alike."
                                        —Robert Frost

"A novel is like a violin-bow. The box which gives off the sounds is the soul of the reader."   —Stendhal

James Thurber's lady leaping into a cartoon, exclaiming, "I come from haunts of coot and hern!"

"[E]very Author, as far as he is great and at the same time original, has had the task of creating the taste by which he is to be enjoyed."   —Wordsworth,
                    Essay Supplemental to the Preface (1815)

"Hope is a good breakfast, but it is a bad supper."
                                        —Sir Francis Bacon

Mae West:
    "Too much of a good thing can be wonderful."
    "When a girl goes bad, men go right after her."
    "Between two evils I always pick the one I never tried before."
    "I generally avoid temptation unless I can't resist it."

Samuel Johnson to Charles Burney:
"And pray, Sir, *who is Bach*? Is he a piper?"

—as nervous as a toad in a mirrored box

Ben Jonson said of Edmund Spenser that he "writ no language." John Berryman, others?

automatic writing / manual drive

"My nature compels me to seek and love things that are well ordered, fleeing confusion, which is as

contrary and inimical to me as is day to the deepest night."
                                        —Nicolas Poussin

Freud: the last Wandering Jew (from his Jewishness)

Kim Novak to Alfred Hitchcock about her character in *Vertigo*: "What's my motivation?"
Hitchcock's reply: "Your paycheck."

G. K. Chesterton: "Nothing improves by translation, save a Bishop."

"To write is always to rave a little . . . There are ways and ways of trumping a thing up: one gets more discriminating, not necessarily more honest."
                    —Elizabeth Bowen, *Death of the Heart*

It was not until prep school that I discovered how to read properly, and I owe the discovery to a madman. At fourteen I started in on the classics. The Jesuits who ran the school are renowned as taskmasters, and that first year we were drilled in declensions and conjugations. By the following year we were considered ready for Homer, and were turned over to the old priest who was to be our guide through the *Odyssey*. As it turned out, several years later he was retired to a mental hospital, but I remain indebted to what were still then merely called his "eccentricities." Each night's homework consisted of a long episode to be read, parsed, translated, and *understood*. And our teacher did not think we could truly understand Homer, or his hero's trials, unless we duplicated the circumstances of the poem. To that end, we were instructed each night to go to the basement of our homes with a lighted candle and a bowl of applesauce—and, between gulped spoonfuls, declaim the Greek, pretending we were in the hold of a storm-tossed ship. I was never, before or since, so enthralled to a text. I now realize that what excited me then was not just the story or the theatrics. It was the words themselves. Because the Greek words were strange, I had to *think* about them, about their sound and etymology, their meanings and overtones, how they were combined into sentences and metaphors. The mad old priest was right: *reading* Homer finally involved the same struggle and search, adventures and homecoming Odysseus himself was driven to.

Another pivotal moment suddenly occurs to me. After my sophomore year at Georgetown, I stayed on in Washington for the summer and enrolled, by special permission, in a graduate seminar on Elizabeth literature. Our textbook was the old Hebel and Hudson *Tudor Poetry and Prose*, a massive, closely printed compendium as stuffy as our professor with his wedge of white hair, steel-rimmed spectacles, and stack of file cards that, having drily relayed the fact or "idea" on each, he would snap like playing cards to the back of the deck. I was intimidated, not by being over my academic head or by his lackluster recital (actually, for reasons I can now neither recall nor imagine, he inspired me to a love of Hooker's *Of the Laws of Ecclesiastical Polity*), but by the enormity and grandeur of the subject. I made of my apartment that summer a context for my study: curling Hilliard and Holbein prints on the wall, Julian Bream plucking Dowland on the stereo set. Still, I was playing at it, accumulating rather than concentrating. Then, one day, the assignment was Christopher Marlowe's "Hero and Leander"...

On Hellespont, guilty of true love's blood,
In view, and opposite, two cities stood,'
Sea-borderers, disjoined by Neptune's might;
The one Abydos, the other Sestos hight.

So the poem begins, and goes on to trace the heavenly path that runs along Leander's back and the pearl-strewn seabed where, stripped to the ivory skin, his body comes to rest. I was literally overwhelmed. It rarely matters who precisely initiates you—the old whore in a walkup, a teenager in the locker room, the telephone lineman picked up at a bar. The experience is decisive. So was this one. It was the first time I had felt the erotic power of a poem. In retrospect, that seems a crucial moment in anyone's reading life: to fall in love with a text, to feel its sexual heat, to sense it unbuttoning your shirt. I cannot resist...quoting a few lines from the poem:

Amorous Leander, beautiful and young,
(Whose tragedy divine Musaeus sung)
Dwelt at Abydos; since him dwelt there none
For whom succeeding times make greater moan.
His dangling tresses that were never shorn,
Had they been cut and unto Colchis borne,
Would have allured the vent'rous youth of Greece
To hazard more than for the Golden Fleece.
Fair Cynthia wished his arms might be her sphere;
Grief makes her pale, because she moves not there.
His body was as straight as Circe's wand;
Jove might have sipped out nectar from his hand.
Even as delicious meat is to the taste,
So was his neck in touching, and surpassed
The white of Pelops' shoulder. I could tell ye
How smooth his breast was, and how white his
    belly,
And whose immortal fingers did imprint
That heavenly path, with many a curious dint
That runs along his back; but my rude pen
Can hardly blazon forth the loves of men,
Much less of powerful gods; let it suffice
That my slack muse sings of Leander's eyes,
Those orient cheeks and lips, exceeding his
That leapt into the water for a kiss
Of his own shadow, and despising many,
Died ere he could enjoy the love of any.
Enamored of his beauty had he been;
His presence made the rudest peasant melt,
That in the vast uplandish country dwelt;
The barbarous Thracian soldier, moved with
    nought,

Was moved with him, and for his favor sought.
Some swore he was a maid in man's attire,
For in his looks were all that men desire:
A pleasant smiling cheek, a speaking eye,
A brow for love to banquet royally;
Leander, thou art made for amorous play;
Why art thou not in love, and loved of all?
Though thou be fair, yet be not thine own thrall.

Stéphane Mallarmé: "the serenity of abstraction"

Aristotle: "History is what Alcibiades did and suffered."

"The dancer Nijinsky was once asked how he managed to leap so high. He is reported to have answered that he saw no great problem in this. Most people when they leapt in the air came down at once. 'Why should you come down immediately? Stay in the air a little before you return, why not?' he is reported to have said. One of the criteria of genius seems to me to be the power to do something perfectly simple and visible which ordinary people cannot, and know they cannot, do—nor do they know how it is done, or why they cannot begin to do it."   —Isaiah Berlin,
Personal Impressions (1981)

In Japan, the living national treasures are called "Holders of Important Intangible Resources."

          ∞

—It's easier to milk a bat than —.
—bitty

          ∞

X leads with his chin.

          ∞

Paul Valéry: poetry is a "prolonged hesitation between sound and sense."

          ∞

—recently dead authors: *les grands disparus*.

          ∞

Roger Shattuck, apropos Phillipe Sollers's novel *Paradis*, refers to "the prestige of obscurity."

          ∞

After the premiere of Tchaikovsky's *Romeo and Juliet*, one disgruntled critic dismissed it as "devoid of melodic invention."

          ∞

"I found the poems in the fields
And only wrote them down."
                    —John Clare, "Sighing for Retirement"

James Schuyler—a plein-air style

Eric Satie: Je suis venu au monde très jeune dans un temps très vieux. [I came into the world very young in a time that was very old.]

Jean Cocteau, *The Difficulty of Being* (1967):
  "I know to what extent I can go too far."

  "Gifts assume the first shape they meet, and this shape might perchance be the right one."

Hostinato rigore ["determined severity"]
                    —motto of Leonardo

"The greatest thing a human soul ever does in this world is to see something, and tell what it saw in a plain way. Hundreds of people can talk for one who can think, but thousands can think for one who can see. To see clearly is poetry, prophecy, and religion—all in one."   —John Ruskin,
            Modern Painters (1856), Volume IV, xv

André Gide called the French language a piano without pedals.

"Erté's letters are 'poetic.' What does this mean? The 'poetic' is not some vague impression, a kind of indefinable value to which we refer conveniently, as an opposition to the 'prosaic.' The 'poetic' is, very exactly, the symbolic capacity of a form; this capacity is valid if it allows the form to 'depart' in a very high number of directions and then to show, potentially, the infinite progression of the symbol, which we can never assign a final meaning and which is finally always the meaning of a new meaning (so that the true antonym of the poetic is not the prosaic, but the stereotype)."   —Roland Barthes on Erté's *Alphabet*,
in *The Responsibility of Forms* (1991)

Katabori — Japanese for "the artist has left no surface untouched."

—Étude de moeurs
—a story "with a twist" — like a martini

"A poet has to live because poetry is nourished by life. But it is not enough to live an interesting or intense life to write good poems. Hundreds of soldiers were at Lepanto; only Cervantes wrote *Don Quixote*; many have been in love; only Petrarch wrote those marvelous sonnets. Poetry is a fate: there is a faculty, perhaps inborn, that leads us to make poems. However, poetry keeps a faith as well. To what? To language. The morality of the poet is verbal: it is loyalty to the word. The poet may be a drunk, a Don Juan, a sponger: that is between him and his conscience. What saves or damns him, as poet, is his relationship with the language. It is a relationship that combines the most rare with the most common feelings: love, friendship, devotion, *camaraderie*, freedom, fun, faithfulness, craftsmanship. The word is the lover and the friend of the poet, his father and his mother, his god and his devil, his hammer and his pillow. It is his enemy too: his mirror." —Octavio Paz, *Revista de la Universidad de Mexico*, #1 (May 1981)

H. L. Menkin called a martini "the only American invention as perfect as a sonnet."

"I composed Tristan under the stress of a great passion and after several months of theoretical meditation." —Richard Wagner

"I am never satisfied that I have handled a subject properly until I have contradicted myself at least three times."   —John Ruskin, in an inaugural address to the Cambridge School of Art in 1858

∞

"Dreamt that I was saying or reading, or that it was read to me, 'Varrius thus prophesied vinegar at his door by damned frigid tremblings.'" —Samuel Taylor Coleridge, letter dated April 8, 1805, in *Anima Poetæ*

∞

"There were some glorious flashes of silence."
—Sydney Smith on Lord Macaulay (once sick in bed)

∞

Charles II's traditional last words: "Let not poor Nelly starve."

∞

—mock-pearls of wisdom

∞

Legal logic: the man who promised he would not drink a drop—so poured his bottle of claret into a loaf of bread, and *ate* it.

Tennyson: "You cannot wonder at my horror of all the libels and slanders; people began to slander me in early days. For example, after my marriage we spent the honeymoon on Coniston Lake in a cottage lent to me by James Marshall. Shortly after this, a paragraph appeared in an American newspaper to the following effect: 'We hope now that Mr. Tennyson is married and is returned to his native lakes, that he will give up opium.'"

"If you were to make little fishes talk, they would talk like whales."   —Oliver Goldsmith to Dr. Johnson

Lord Byron had (so he said) a paper in which were folded locks of hair from Lucretia Borgia, John Milton, Napoleon Buonaparte, and Dr. Johnson.

"Always, sir, manage to have at your table some fleshy, blooming young writer or cadet, just come out, that the mosquitoes may stick to him and leave the rest of the company alone."   —Bobus Smith (brother of Sydney), advice to Lord Macaulay

"Upon hearing a celebrated performer go through a hard composition, and hearing it remarked that it was very difficult, Dr. Johnson said, 'I would it had been impossible.'" —Boswell

＊

"Another damned thick square book! Always scribble, scribble, scribble! Eh, Mr. Gibbon?" —William Henry, Duke of Gloucester (brother of King George III), upon being presented the second volume of Gibbon's *Decline and Fall of the Roman Empire*

＊

—*marchand de modes* [shopkeeper]

＊

Cromwell: "Take away that bauble."

＊

In *The Vicar of Wakefield*, Oliver Goldsmith suggests that the art of the cognoscenti is easily acquired: "The whole secret consists in a strict adherence to two rules: the one, always to observe that the picture might have been better if the painter had taken more pains; and the other, to praise the works of Pietro Perusino."

＊

—The weather is here. Wish you were beautiful. Etc.
—we exchanged unpleasantries

—echo—taking dictation

"He saw nature through the spectacles of books."
—Dr. Johnson on John Milton

"Last Sunday I took a walk towards Highgate, and in the lane that winds by the side of Lord Mansfield's park I met Mr. Green our Demonstrator at Guy's in conversation with Coleridge—I joined them, after enquiring by a look whether it would be agreeable—I walked with him at his alderman-after-dinner pace for near two miles I suppose. In those two miles he broached a thousand things—let me see if I can give you a list—Nightingales—Poetry—on Poetical Sensation—Metaphysics—Different genera and species of Dreams—Nightmares—a dream accompanied by a sense of touch—single and double touch—a dream related—first and second consciousness—the difference explained between will and volition—so say metaphysicians from a want of smoking the second consciousness—Monsters—the Kraken—Mermaids—Southey believes in them—Southey's belief too much diluted—a Ghost story—Good morning— I heard his voice as he came towards me—I heard it as he moved away—I heard it all the interval—if it may be called so. He was civil enough to ask me to call on him at Highgate."   —John Keats,
in an April 1819 letter to his brother,
about a meeting with Samuel Taylor Coleridge

X's style is pulled backward through a mangle.

—the "brag" (of colors, images, etc.)

"When Japanese aestheticians spoke of the quality of things known as wabi, they had in mind something like this: *the perfect nature of humble ordinary objects, seen for themselves, in a state of unfussed clarity*. Chardin had this most of the time, and Vermeer nearly all of it; Manet and Georges Braque, in very different ways, understood it; and Morandi's entire life was predicated on the prolonged search for it. That is why the Guggenheim's show provides such a wonderful lesson in seeing, a metaphysical oasis in the ballyhoo and braggadocio of late modernism."
                        —Robert Hughes in *Time* magazine

"Contemporary trends of thought imagine that art is a fountain, whereas it is a sponge. They have decided that art should gush forth, whereas it should absorb and become saturated. They think it can be broken down into methods of depiction, whereas it is composed of organs of perception. The proper task of art is to be always an observer, to gauge more purely than others do, more receptively and faithfully."
                        —Boris Pasternak

George Bernard Shaw was irritated by praise of his style in music criticism. It made him feel like a man who shouted "Fire!" to people who responded by saying, "How admirably laconic!"

une veuve abusive — the sort of conventionally aggressive widow who throws a wet blanket of respectability over any significant irregularities in her late husband's thought or behavior.

"The Dream is a second life."—Gérard de Nerval,
Aurelia (1855), opening sentence

—The Big Cats at feeding time.

Mao—the most popular contemporary poet (nearly a billion fans)—and so quickly out of fashion.

According to John B. Carroll, Peter Davies and Barry Rickman in *The American Heritage Word Frequency Book* (1971), the five most common nouns in English are (in order) *time, people, way, water, words.*

The most frequent words: *the, of, and, a, too.*
The most frequent letters: E, T, A, O, I, N, S, H, R, D, L, U.

Myths (like math) are figurative narratives about relationships and exchanges of energy (power). Characters are functions: discharging resources (Wrath-
ful Father, Avenging Son, Devouring Monsters), key
exchanges (Messenger, Warrior, Beloved), etc. Just
as numbers articulate "abstract" relationships in
nature's design and quantity. Types of relationships
(power): love, hate, revenge. Situations: Discovery After Long Time Quest—the most abstract of all
myths.

"All eight-year-olds have genius—except Minou
Drouet."
                                              —Jean Cocteau

"What kind of times are they, when
A talk about trees is almost a crime
Because it implies silence about so many horrors?"
                    —Bertolt Brecht, "To Those Born Later"

"Whatever satisfies the soul is truth."
                              —Walt Whitman, 1855 Preface

—rhyme like cufflinks
—the critic as Beckmesser
—hash Browning
—worth its wait in gold (of a jewel?)
—eye-stabbing

"Nobody has been converted to Christianity by reading Dante. Art does not make peace, that is not its
task; art is peace."   —Robert Lowell,
                a few weeks before his death, in Moscow

—surprise by a fine excess

Novalis, on Romantic art: "To make the familiar
strange, and the strange familiar."

—new thresholds, new anatomies
—rope-trick
—shelf-life

"Wagner's music is better than it sounds."
                                —Mark Twain

"A cauliflower is a cabbage with a college education."
                          —Mark Twain, *Pudd'nhead Wilson*

—minatory
—thrice-distilled

"I soared, at first, quite out of Reason's view,
And now am lost above it."   —Cleopatra,
                          in John Dryden's *All for Love* (1677)

"The moving Toyshop of the Heart"
                          —Alexander Pope, "The Rape of the Lock"

"The foul rag-and-bone shop of the heart"
          —W. B. Yeats, "The Circus Animals' Desertion"

"I alone of English writers have consciously set
myself to make music out of what I may call the
sound of sense."   —Robert Frost,
                          in a letter to John Bartlett, July 4, 1913

"Poetry is an extravagance about grief."
                          —Robert Frost

"It's my masterpiece. Unfortunately, it contains no
music."   —Maurice Ravel, on his *Bolero*

The aim of literature, Roland Barthes asserts, is to
put "meaning" into the world but not "a meaning."
Mightn't writing students be urged to try for this
when they put a poem together. Barthes further distinguishes between a work's "message" and its "system" (e.g., form, structure).

"I don't paint things, I only paint differences between things."   —Matisse

Workshops have made the university safe for poetry.

—Where are our "liberating gods" (Ralph Waldo Emerson)?
—"junk poetry" like junk food
—Round up the usual suspects.
—the critic-as-curator
—X's style is churriqueresque
—jacqueril
—loupe (under the jeweler's loupe, the diamond
proves to be paste)

Owen Barfield's test of a poet—what words, having read him, do I use with an extended meaning?

"Art does not render the visible but renders visible."
                                                    —Paul Klee

Stravinsky said the guitar sounds not small but as from far away.

Haiku as High Coo

Robert Craft refers to someone (Kyra Nijinsky, in fact) as "an incontinent reminiscer" (in "My Life with Stravinsky," *New York Review of Books*, June 10, 1982)

—clever-boots

. . . there's smoke up his dragon's nostrils.

"I see them all, so excellently fair,
I see, not feel, how beautiful they are!"
                              —Samuel Taylor Coleridge,
                              "Dejection: An Ode" (1802)

"I love to see, when leaves depart,
The clear anatomy arrive,
Winter, the paragon of art,
That kills all forms of life and feeling
Save what is pure and will survive."
                              —Roy Campbell, "Autumn"

"The truth of an idea is not a stagnant property inherent in it. Truth *happens* to an idea. It *becomes* true,
is *made* true by events. . . ."
        —William James, *The Meaning of Truth* (1909)

" . . . truth [is] something essentially bound up with
the way in which one moment in our experience
may lead us towards other moments which it will be
worthwhile to have been led to."
                    —William James, *Pragmatism* (1907)

"So here we are, whether we like it or not, in the
realm of necessity. And yet which of us has ever heard
talk of art as other than a realm of freedom? This
sort of heresy is uniformly widespread because it is

imagined that art is outside the bounds of ordinary activity. Well, in art as in everything else, one can build only upon a resisting foundation; whatever constantly gives way to pressure constantly renders movement impossible."

—Igor Stravinsky, *The Poetics of Music*

"*How They Brought the Good News from Aix to Ghent* (at about age nine). I thought it was pretty nearly the height of human achievement. I didn't know whether I was impressed by riding a horse that fast or writing the poem. I couldn't distinguish between the two, but I knew there was something pretty fine going on. . . . Then *Lycidas* . . . By thirteen, something like that, I knew it wasn't what was happening in the poem that was important—it was the poem. I had crossed the line."

—Robert Penn Warren

—X is the Fretful Porpentine.
—bubbling stem
—unbuttoned
—the fellahin
—earwig
—behemoth

"I cannot see the man for the likeness."

—Roger Fry's comment on a portrait by Sargent

Margot Asquith:

"Lord Birkenhead is very clever, but sometimes his brains go to his head."

"The Bible tells us to forgive our enemies; not our friends."

"The room smelt of not having been smoked in."
                                        —Ronald Knox

The story of the Master of Trinity College, waking up at a college meeting and remarking, "A strong case, tellingly put."

". . . the phrase always seems to me to pause and slowly pivot upon itself."
                                —Henry James said of Tennyson's style

"Good taste is the ability continuously to counteract exaggeration. Each epoch has its own sentimentality, its specific way of overemphasizing strata of emotion. The sentimentality of the present is egotistic and un-loving; it exaggerates not the feeling of love but that of the self."
                —Hugo von Hofmannsthal, *Book of Friends* (1922)

As Auden put it in his introduction to a school's anthology of 1935 (*The Poet's Tongue*) poetry is "memorable speech": "About what? Birth, death, the Beatific Vision, the abysses of hatred and fear, the awards and miseries of desire, the unjust walking the earth and the just scratching miserably for food like hens, triumphs, earthquakes, deserts of boredom and featureless anxiety, the Golden Age promised or irrevocably past, the gratifications and terrors of childhood, the impact of nature on the adolescent, the despairs and wisdoms of the mature, the sacrificial victim, the descent into Hell, the devouring and the benign mother? Yes, all of these, but not these only. Everything that we remember, no matter how trivial: the mark on the wall, the joke at luncheon, word games, these, like the dance of a stoat or the raven's gamble, are equally the subject of poetry.

"We shall do poetry a great disservice if we confine it only to the major experiences of life. . . ."

X bit off more than he could eschew.

"The most stupendous scenery ceases to be sublime when it becomes distinct, or in other words limited, and the imagination is no longer encouraged to exaggerate it." —Henry David Thoreau,
A Week on the Concord and Merrimack Rivers (1849)

"Why do I employ sprung rhythm at all? Because it is the nearest to the rhythm of prose, that is the native and natural rhythm of speech, the least forced, the most rhetorical and emphatic of all possible rhythms, combining, as it seems to me, opposite and, one wd. have thought, incompatible excellences, markedness of rhythm—that is rhythm's self— and naturalness of expression . . ." —Gerard Manley Hopkins, letter to Robert Bridges, August 21, 1877

Gerard Manley Hopkins's grandfather was a surgeon, a fellow student of Keats.

Léger was a student of Gérôme.

"For it seems to me that the poetical language of an age shd. be the current language, heightened, to any degree heightened and unlike itself, but not (I mean normally: passing freaks and graces are another thing) an obsolete one.   —Gerard Manley Hopkins, letter to Robert Bridges, August 14, 1879

Lowell wrote up to his talent. Berryman wrote down to his. Jarrell did the intelligent best he could with a minor talent.

"The enlightened goodwill of men acting in an individual capacity is the only possible principle of social progress; if social necessities, once clearly perceived, were found to lie outside the range of this goodwill in the same way as those which govern the stars, each man would have nothing more to do but to watch history unfolding as one watches the seasons go by, while doing his best to spare himself and his loved ones the misfortune of being either an instrument or a victim of social oppression."　　—Simone Weil, "Analysis of Oppression"

"Thou swell, thou witty, thou sweet, thou grand."
　　　　　　　　　　　　　　　—Lorenz Hart lyric

Nothing is more *logical* than a dream.

Henry David Thoreau, *A Week on the Concord and Merrimack Rivers* (1849):
　　"This seems a long while ago, and yet it happened since Milton wrote his *Paradise Lost*."

Thoreau quotes Goethe from *Dichtung und Wahrheit*: "I had lived among painters from my childhood, and had accustomed myself to look at objects, as they did, with reference to art."

"A man cannot wheedle nor overawe his Genius."

"The poet is no tender slip of fairy stock, who requires peculiar institutions and edicts for his defense, but the toughest son of earth and of Heaven, and by his greater strength and endurance his fainting companions will recognize the God in him. It is the worshippers of beauty, after all, who have done the real pioneer work of the world."

"Great men, unknown to their generation, have their fame among the great who have preceded them, and all true worldly fame subsides from their high estimate beyond the stars."

∞

—wormeaten
—voluptuary acolyte

∞

Toute societé est un édifice d'enchantements.
[All of society is an edifice of enchantments.]
                                                —Paul Valéry

∞

Box and Cox — vaudeville team.

Para ir al infierno, no hace falta cambiar de sitio ni postura. [To go to hell, one need never change place or position.]
                                                    —Rafael Alberti

—dead heat
—anathemas
—pirate

Maybe I'd send it a drink. But I wouldn't cross the room to talk to it.

Poetry has been legislated unacknowledgment.

"Au fond de l'inconnu pour trouver du nouveau!" [Go to the bottom of the unknown in order to discover the new!]
                                            —Charles Baudelaire,
                                    last line of "L'Invitation au Voyage"

"Reading is a pernicious habit. It destroys all originality of sentiment."
                                                    —Thomas Hobbes

Wilde preferred boys from the lower class because they were "all body and no soul."

"Perversity consists in using one's mind where one's body would suffice."   —Paul Valéry

"Our doubt is our passion, and our passion is our task."
                                                    —Henry James

R. P. Blackmur considered medieval music "the ultimate art" because it was "incredibly the least committed to any prejudice or experience except itself."

"The purpose of art is to lay bare the questions hidden by the answers."   —James Baldwin

Richard Howard quotes Alain Robbe-Grillet as remarking: In classical times, a man told a story he knew to an audience who also knew it; then, from the Middle Ages through the nineteenth century, the

James

3 Bolton St. W.
April 29th

Dear Sir.

I am much obliged
to you for the two & tall
all the Lyceum tonight,
which I will make
use I write much
pleasure. Very truly H. James

man told a story he knew to an audience that did not know it; since then, he's told a story he doesn't know to an audience that doesn't know it either.

※

"I thought to erect a minor monument of language on the menacing shore of the ocean of gibberish."
—Paul Valéry

※

"L'Art, c'est le désir perpetué."
[Art is the perpetuation of desire.]
—Jules Laforgue

※

In *Le Traité du Narcisse* (1891) Gide says: "Everything has been said before, but since nobody listens we have to keep going back and beginning all over again."

※

—The banana republic of poets-in-translation.
—quarrelsome as a gull

※

"Our interest's on the dangerous edge of things."
—Robert Browning, "Bishop Blougram's Apology"
(1855)

"There were more beautiful women in Greece than Helen; but what of them?"   —Thomas Hardy

—Easier done than said.

John Clare: "I wrote because it pleased me in sorrow, and when I am happy it makes me more happy and so I go on."

"Thomas Gray walks as if he had fouled his small-clothes and looks as if he smelt it."

— Christopher Smart

Knollenstils—exaggerated,   grotesque   musculature (Hendrik Goltzius)

"I have made a sketch of a sunset . . . and now would like to have the opportunity to see a number of good pictures so that I can become more dissatisfied with my own work. Only in such circumstances can I be certain of making progress. . . ."   —Igor Stravinsky, in a letter to his parents as a teenager

"What do I want to communicate but what a *hell* of a good time I had writing it." —Robert Frost to Richard Poirier, *The Paris Review* interview (Issue 24, Summer-Fall 1960)

There was a wall of communication between them.

"The miniature does not derive from the dimension but from a kind of precision which the thing observes in delimiting itself stopping, finishing."
—Roland Barthes, *Empire of Signs* (1983)

—pièce montée
—faisandé – (meat left to rot) – gamy
—acharya – Sanskrit for "teacher"
—Kraken
—genere fantastico
—X is a back number

"Now that his writing has improved, we have been able to discover how little he knows." —from the conclusion of a boy's report in an English prep school

In an interview, Christopher Isherwood recalled a Stephen Spender story about Yeats—"that he went for days on end without noticing anything, but then, about once a month, he would look out of the window and suddenly be aware of a swan or something, and it gave him such a stunning shock that he'd write a marvelous poem about it."

"*Horizon* will always publish stories of pure realism, but we take the line that experiences connected with the blitz, the shopping queues, the home front, deserted wives, deceived husbands, broken homes, dull jobs, bad schools, group squabbles, are so much a picture of our ordinary lives that unless the workmanship is outstanding we are against them."
—Cyril Connolly, 1944

When an anecdote is not just *ben trovato*, but *troppo ben trovato*.

"He has brains in his Head, which is all the more interesting for a little twist in the Brains."
—Samuel Taylor Coleridge in a March 10th, 1804 letter on Sir Thomas Browne

"To sing the blues you have to live it. I can sing about my mule being stolen, so I don't have no way of actually getting my vegetables to the market, because that actually happened to me, but I can't sing about a bomb dropping on my house, they can do that in Europe, and that would be their blues."

—Big Bill Broonzy

The "Mysterians" —Arlene Croce's term for Robert Wilson, Lucinda Childs, Philip Glass, etc.

Tenui musam meditamur avena. [We cultivate literature on a little oatmeal.]

—motto of Sydney Smith's *Edinburgh Review*

Dr. Johnson:

"No man but a blockhead ever wrote, except for money."

"Read over your composition, and where ever you meet with a passage which you think is particularly fine, strike it out."

"Criticism is a study by which men grow important and formidable at a very small expense."

"Milton was a genius that could cut a Colossus from a rock but could not carve heads upon cherry-stones."

"When I take up the end of a web, and find it pack-thread, I do not expect by looking further, to find embroidery."

Sydney Smith:
"I have no relish for the country: it is a sort of healthy grave."

"You remember Thurlow's answer to someone complaining of the injustice of a company. 'Why, you never expected justice from a company, did you? They have neither a soul to lose nor a body to kick."

Nec tamen ut testes mos est audire poetas. [Nor is it customary to listen to poets like sworn witnesses.]
—Ovid, Elegy XII

Auden said it is bad manners not to be boring occasionally.

William Congreve, *The Way of the World* (1700):
"Last night was one of their cabal nights; they have 'em three times-a-week, and meet by turns at one another's apartments, where they come together like the coroner's inquest, to sit upon the murdered reputations of the week." (Fainall, Act I, Scene I)

". . . and you know she [Lady Wishfort] hates Mirabell worse than a quaker hates a parrot." (Witwoud, Act I, Scene IX)

Act III, Scene V:
Lady Wishfort: "Let me see the glass.—Cracks, sayest thou?—why, I am arrantly flayed—I look like an old peeled wall. Thou must repair me, Foible, before Sir Rowland comes, or I shall never keep up to my picture."

Foible: "I warrant you, madam, a little art once made your picture like you, and now a little of the same art must make you like your picture. Your picture must sit for you, madam."

"She has a month's mind." (Foible, Act III, Scene VI)

". . . fools never wear out—they are such *drop de Berri* things!" (Mrs. Millimant, Act III, Scene III)

"What, are you all got together, like players at the end of the last act?" (Witwoud, Act V, Scene III)

". . . genuine and authorized tea-table talk—such as mending of fashions, spoiling reputations, railing at absent friends, and so forth—" (Mirabell, Act IV, Scene I)

—a rusalka

Peter De Vries once said his ambition was to have a mass audience large enough for his select following to despise.

X is a rhinoceros, not a unicorn.

"sorcellerie évocatoire"   —Baudelaire

On the inside lid of the virginal I commissioned to be built for me by the great David Way, I had a motto painted:

DUM VIXI TACUI
MORTUA DULCE CANO

It was said to have been inscribed on the tortoise shell Apollo first used as his lyre. The shell—or now, this instrument's wood—is speaking: "While I was alive, I was silent. Now that I am dead, I sing sweetly."

Coleridge's warning against similes: "a perpetual trick of moralizing everything."

Dante's palindrome: "In girum imus nocte et con-
sumimur igni." Because of its imbricate complexity,
any palindrome is nearly impossible to translate.
This one seems to mean: "we go in a circle at night,
and we are consumed by fire." That implies it is also
a riddle, whose answer to the implicit "who am I?" is
the stars.

"Dryden's genius was of the sort which catches fire by
its own motion; his chariot wheels get hot by driving
fast."   —Samuel Taylor Coleridge,
                        Table Talk, November 1, 1833

"In our case, there will be no 'replacement.' A reper-
tory, a patrimony of ballets, tended as carefully as the
collection of 600-year-old bonsai in Tokyo's Imperial
Palace conservatory, is not replaced; it is preserved,
maintained, refreshed to give rebirth by grafting and
seedlings. The expression of a sensibility is present
as a continuum, to be seized upon by important pos-
sibilities."   —Lincoln Kirstein,
            on the NYC Ballet, *New York Times*, 17 Mar 1983

To "list" once meant not just to document or itemize
but to love and desire.

Planets in the night sky are "vagabond stars."

"Please tell Mr. Eisenstein that I have seen his film *Potemkin* and admire it very much. What we should like would be for him to do something of the same kind, but rather cheaper, for Ronald Colman."
—Samuel L. Goldwyn

"We have complicated all the simple gifts of the gods."
—Heraclitus

"Perhaps you should say something
A bit more interesting than what you mean."
—Peter Porter

"We know our poem by its being the only poem."
—Isaac Rosenberg, in a fragmentary essay on Emerson

qui s'excuse s'accuse. (Christopher Ricks: qui s'accuse s'accuse)

sutra: "précepte sanskrit condensé en un style lapi-
daire" [a Sanskrit precept condensed in a lapidary
style]   —*Le Grand Robert*

"Somebody's boring me. . . . I think it's me."
                                    —Dylan Thomas

"Read at whim! Read at whim!"   —Randall Jarrell

"Dejection of Spirits, which I suppose may have prevented many a man from becoming an Author, made
me one."   —William Cowper,
              letter to his cousin Harriet Hesketh

Roy Campbell, in his 1946 *Talking Bronco*, invented
the term "the MacSpaunday group" for the 1930's
gang of poets.

Only the mediocre are always at their best.
                                    —Jean Giraudoux

Nicolas Poussin—The Classical Ideal—The Golden
Mean

It was a quest pursuing the invisible where, as in stark
darkness, no step was taken without support.

The Supports: Vitruvius' six principles governing architecture (order, arrangement, symmetry, eurhyth-
my, economy, propriety); Aristotle's six principles
governing tragedy (plot, character, diction, thought,
spectacle, song); and Cicero's three principles governing rhetoric (invention, disposition, elocution).
The *real* is subjected to laws of harmony, and to Chris-
tian doctrine (theology combined with rhetoric).

Theory of Modes. *Modus*: "measure which one
should not exceed." Poussin links it with modesty
(médiocrité) and moderation. Each Mode is subor-
dinated to a dominant, which applies equally to music, architecture, theater, and the visual arts. Doric/
tragedy, Ionian/comedy, Corinthian/satire . . .

There are two classes of Modes:

1. "very joyful and lively"; CFG; melodic intervals
are without semitones; expresses asprezza, durezza,
crudeltà, amaritudine.

2. "rather sad"; DEA; with semitones; piano, do-
lore, cordoglio, sospiri, lagrime.

Robert Creeley's line is anorectic.

—full-rigged
—swill

Philip Glass's idiom is called "motoric arpeggiation," running patterns repeated and juxtaposed.

The baby boom: there are so many young poets these days, one expects suicide notes that read "Done because we are too menny," as in Hardy's *Jude the Obscure*.

"I'm sure that you'd like to know how I feel about Proust. That's the first thing people ask me. My feeling about Proust. It is generally supposed that I had my qualms about Proust. On the contrary, I was a very fervent admirer of Proust and when people keep on saying that I turned down *Swann* at Gallimard's they forget that one is busy, that one simply can't read *everything*, and Proust had this aura of a faded social butterfly."   —André Gide, quoted in
Frederic Prokosch's *Voices: A Memoir* (1983)

"Sentences must stir in a book like leaves in a forest, each distinct from each, despite their resemblance."
—Gustave Flaubert

"Love will make you do things
That you know is wrong."
—Billie Holiday, "Fine and Mellow"

"The sublime in art is the attempt to express the infinite without finding in the realm of phenomena any object which proves itself fitting for this representation."
—Georg Wilhelm Hegel

"There are no longer any laws, merely conventions: nothing but form." —Vautrin to Lucien de Rubempré, to save him from suicide in Balzac's *Lost Illusions*

"Never have I had more ideas about art in my head, and yet I am forced to do flowers. This cannot go on."
—Henri Fantin-Latour, 1862

—Simple Simonism

"Words know about us things we do not know about
ourselves."   —René Char

"I didn't like it. He has such a noisy spiritual life."
—Artur Schnabel on a famous fellow-pianist's recital

"I perhaps heard a voice, a deeply moving contralto.
That voice must have put me in a state such as nothing
had suggested to me before. . . . And I took it unknow-
ingly as a measure of psychological states, and have
striven all my life to make, find, think something that
might directly revive in me, force from me—in accord
with this *chance song*—the real, necessary, absolute
thing for which from my childhood, this *forgotten
song* had prepared a niche."   —Paul Valéry
              (Valéry wrote for a particular voice)

"It seems to me there is nothing so valuable for getting one's ideas clear as to write a long and obscure
poem."   —Paul Valéry

"You might call it a kind of automatic writing carried
out in a state of total consciousness. . . . I am now convinced that in a work of art we do not try to conjure up

beauty or truth. We only have recourse to them—as to a subterfuge—in order to be able to go on breathing."
—Robert Pinget, on his writing

"I like Mr. Stevens' things when they are not affected, but he writes so much that is affected."—Elsie Stevens

"Why attack God? He may be as unhappy as we are."
—Erik Satie

"Look for a long time at what pleases you, and longer still at what pains you."   —Colette

"A poet is a nasty cur even when he isn't having a fit."
—Ford Madox Ford's translation of
"poeta nascitur, non fit"

Edwin Denby called dance "the formal world of civilized fantasy."

"Dear Elias: When I speak of the poem, or often when I speak of the poem, in this book, I mean not merely a literary form, but the brightest and most harmonious concept, or order, of life; and the references should be read with that in mind." —Wallace Stevens' inscription in Elias Mengel's copy of *Collected Poems*

"I don't want you to understand them, just learn the damn things!"   —Ezra Pound to Mary de Rachewiltz, struggling with the *Cantos*

— psychophant
— fan de siècle
— a slash of gin

"Only mediocrities develop."   —Oscar Wilde

Auden said the poet's job is to find out the images "that hurt and connect."

"In Hollywood we acquire the finest novels in order to smell their leather bindings."   —Ernst Lubitsch

¢ Hartford Accident & Ind. Co.
690 Asylum Avenue
Hartford, Conn.

Miss Anna M. Wirtz
142 Edwards Street
New Haven, Conn.

Dear Miss Wirtz:

    Some time ago I made up my mind not
to explain poems, because the meaning of the poem
is merely a part of it.

    Of course, I never meant that ice
cream is, for good and all, the _summum bonum_.   If
the meaning of a poem was its essential characteristic,
people would be putting themselves to a lot of trouble
about nothing to set the meaning in a poetic form.

                    Very truly yours,

"There are two kinds of taste, the taste for emotions of surprise and the taste for emotions of recognition."
—Henry James

"He who is not in some measure a pedant, though he may be wise, cannot be a very happy man."
—William Hazlitt

"Love's of itself, too sweet; the best of all
Is, when love's honey has a dash of gall."
—Robert Herrick

"Baghdad on the Hudson"
— O. Henry's phrase for New York City

Auden: a poem has "an immediate meaning and a possible meaning."

"The great writer is always the plodder; it's the ephemeral writer that has to get on with the job."
—Ezra Pound

"Shame the eager with ironic praise."
—Alexander Pope

Auden's poem "The Quest," echoing Pope:
  "To test the resolution of the young
  With tales of the small failings of the great,
  And shame the eager with ironic praise."

"Ultimately, there is something odd about settling in somewhere new—about the perhaps laborious process of getting used to new surroundings and fitting in, a task we undertake almost for its own sake and with the definite intention of abandoning the place again as soon as it is accomplished, or shortly thereafter, and returning to our previous state. We insert that sort of thing into the mainstream of our lives as a kind of interruption or interlude, for the purpose of 'recreation,' which is to say: a refreshing, revitalizing exercise of the organism, because it was in immediate danger of overindulging itself in the uninterrupted monotony of daily life, of languishing and growing indifferent. And what is the cause of the enervation and apathy that arise when the rules of life are not abrogated from time to time? It is not so much the physical and mental exhaustion and abrasion that come with the challenges of life (for these, in fact, simple rest would be the best medicine); the cause is, rather, something psychological, our very sense of time itself—which, if it flows with uninterrupted regularity, threatens to elude us and which is so closely related to and bound up with our sense of life that the one sense cannot be weakened without the second's experiencing pain and injury. A great many false ideas have been spread about the nature of boredom.

It is generally believed that by filling time with things new and interesting, we can make it 'pass.' By which we mean 'shorten' it; monotony and emptiness, however, are said to weigh down and hinder its passage. This is not true under all conditions. Emptiness and monotony may stretch a moment or even an hour and make it 'boring,' but they can likewise abbreviate and dissolve large, indeed the largest units of time, until they seem nothing at all. Conversely, rich and interesting events are capable of filling time, until hours, even days, are shortened and speed past on wings; whereas on a larger scale, interest lends the passage of time breadth, solidity, and weight, so that years rich in events pass much more slowly than do paltry, bare, featherweight years that are blown before the wind and are gone. What people call boredom is actually an abnormal compression of time caused by monotony—uninterrupted uniformity can shrink large spaces of time until the heart falters, terrified to death. When one day is like every other, then all days are like one, and perfect homogeneity would make the longest life seem very short, as if it had flown by in a twinkling. Habit arises when our sense of time falls asleep, or at least, grows dull; and if the years of youth are experienced slowly, while the later years of life hurtle past at an ever-increasing speed, it must be habit that causes it. We know full well that the insertion of new habits or the changing of old ones is the only way to preserve life, to renew our sense of time, to rejuvenate, intensify, and retard our experience of time—and thereby renew our sense of life itself. That is the reason for every change of scenery and air, for a trip to the shore: the experience of a variety of refreshing episodes. The first few days in a new place have a youthful swing to them, a kind of sturdy, long stride—that lasts about six to eight days. Then, to the extent that we 'settle in,' that gradual shortening becomes noticeable. Whoever clings to life, or better, wants to cling to life, may realize to his horror that the days have begun to grow light again and are scurrying past; and the last week—of, let us say, four—is uncanny in its fleeting transience. To be sure, this refreshment of our sense of time extends beyond the interlude; its effect is noticeable again when we return to our daily routine. The first few days at home after a change of scene are likewise experienced in a new, broad, more youthful fashion—but only a very few, for we are quicker to grow accustomed to the old rules than to their abrogation. And if our sense of time has grown weary with age or was never all that strongly developed—a sign of an inborn lack of vitality—it very soon falls asleep again, and within twenty-four hours it is as if we were never gone and our journey were merely last night's dream."

—Thomas Mann, *The Magic Mountain*

"Writing was a bore because it was only a means of becoming known and invited out, a preliminary to the serious job of spell-binding."

—Auden about Oscar Wilde

"an almost primitive simplicity of phrase"
　　　　—T. S. Eliot, praising Marianne Moore's *Poems*,
　　　　　　　in *The Dial*, issue 75, December 1923

"Endless curiosity, observation, and a great amount of joy in the thing." —George Grosz, about painting and drawing (according to Marianne Moore in a letter to Mary Markwick Moore Reeves, August 28, 1963)

"A wise woman never yields by appointment."
　　　　　　　　　　　　　　　　—Stendhal

"Marriage is a covered dish."　　　　　—Swiss proverb

"If you are afraid of loneliness, don't marry."
　　　　　　　　　　　　　　　　—Chekhov

"So many good ones; and so many bad ones; that's what you get for trying." —last words of Dutch Schultz

"I'm afraid I am more interested, Mr. Connolly, in the Dublin street names than in the riddle of the universe."　　　　　　　　　　　—James Joyce

"Every opportunity . . . should be taken to discountenance that false and vulgar opinion that rules are the fetters of genius. They are fetters only to men of no genius; as that armour, which upon the strong becomes an ornament and a defense, upon the weak and misshapen turns into a load, and cripples the body which it was made to protect." —Sir Joshua Reynolds
(First of seven *Discourses on Art*, delivered by Reynolds, then President, at the opening of the Royal Academy, January 2, 1769)

"It is art that *makes* life, makes interest, makes importance, for our consideration and application of these things, and I know of no substitute whatever for the force and beauty of its process."
—Henry James, letter to H. G. Wells

"*All* must have prizes," said the Dodo. (*Alice in Wonderland*)

"You are in the streets of a large town, newspapers have just arrived hot from the press—important news—the assassination of a great statesman. You rush to pick one up, agog at this news and overcome with the desire to know more. If, at the very moment you grab hold of the newspaper, you are not equally aware of the smell of fresh printer's ink and the scene of the trees above your head, it's tantamount to not feeling this thing called poetry."　　—Francis Ponge

". . . I would rejoice in it more
If I knew more clearly what
We wanted the knowledge for . . ."
　　　—W. H. Auden, "After Reading a Child's Guide to Modern Physics" (*The New Yorker*, Nov. 17, 1962)

"You are content with little, in fact you do nothing at all, if to express greatness you only use the word greatness."　　　　　　—Francis Ponge

Tacitus's verdict on the Emperor Galba: Omnium consensu capax imperii nisi imperasset [By general consent fit to rule, had he not ruled].

Arnold Schoenberg's transcription of "The Emperor Waltz" for clarinet, violin, cello and harmonium—an image for translation?

"I have been formed in part, and in greater and lesser ways, by all of the music I have known and loved, and I composed as I was formed to compose."

—Igor Stravinsky

Richard Wagner: "deeds of music made visible."

The Japanese ideogram for "noise" is the ideogram for "woman" repeated three times.

"The French, my dear, are hardly white."

—W. H. Auden to Igor Stravinsky

—rust-proof
—X has floured his sauce.

"For a mind of such agility, and for a sensibility so reticent, the minor subject, such as a pleasant little sand-colored skipping animal, may be the best release for the major emotions. . . . We all have to choose whatever subject-matter allows us the most powerful and most secret release; and that is a personal affair."

—T. S. Eliot in his introduction
to Marianne Moore's Selected Poems (1935)

Socrates says (in the *Phaedrus*) that a man is not to be considered a master of harmony simply because he knows how to produce the highest possible note and the lowest possible on his strings.

"Attention is the natural prayer of the soul."
—Nicolas Malebranche

Marianne Moore:

One of the last times Miss Moore was quoted to the press, she was observed taking her advanced age with equanimity: "I'm all bone," she told a visitor in 1967, "just solid, pure bone. I'm good-natured, but hideous as an old hop toad. I look like a scarecrow, like Lazarus awakening. I look permanently alarmed."

"I aspire to be neat. I try to do my hair with a lot of thought to avoid those explosive sunbursts, but when one hairpin goes in, another comes out."

"My physiognomy isn't at all classic. It's like a banana-nosed monkey. Well, I do seem at least to be awake, don't I?"

"We have no knowledge, that is, no general principles drawn from the contemplation of particular facts, but what has been built up by pleasure, and exists in us by pleasure alone. . . . The knowledge both of the Poet and the Man of Science is pleasure."

—William Wordsworth,
1802 Preface to the *Lyrical Ballads*

"If you don't have anything good to say about anybody, come sit beside me."   —Alice Roosevelt Longworth

In P. G. Wodehouse's novel *Much Obliged, Jeeves* (1971), when Bertie Wooster is asked, by Ginger Winship, if he had read Florence Craye's *Spindrift*, he replies: " 'Couldn't put it down,' cunningly not revealing that I hadn't been able to take it up."

"Wilde is not so much borrowed from as contributed to."   —Princess Elizabeth Bibesco,
about Ivy Compton-Burnett's style (in her review of the latter's 1933 novel *More Women than Men*)

"Entre deux mots il faut choisir le moindre."
[The lesser word is always to be preferred.]
—Paul Valéry

Frederick II's invitation to Voltaire:

$$\frac{P}{venez} \; à \; \frac{ci}{100}$$

"Against criticism we can neither protect nor defend ourselves; we must act in despite of it, and gradually it resigns itself to this."
—Goethe

"There are some things I will never discuss, not even with myself."
—Katharine Hepburn

"The most intolerable people are provincial celebrities."
—Anton Chekhov

"During periods of crisis, positions which are false or feigned are very common. Entire generations falsify themselves to themselves; that is to say, they wrap themselves up in artistic styles, in doctrines, in political movements which are insincere, and which fill the lack of genuine convictions. When they get to be about 40 years old, those generations become null and void,

because at that age one can no longer live on fictions."
—José Ortega y Gasset, *Man and Crisis* (1958)

"By all means let a poet, if he wants to, write engagé poems, protesting against this or that political evil or social injustice. But let him remember this. The only person who will benefit from them is himself; they will enhance his literary reputation among those who feel as he does. The evil of injustice, however, will remain exactly what it would have been if he had kept his mouth shut."
—W. H. Auden, "The Public v. the Late Mr. William Butler Yeats" (*Partisan Review*, Spring 1939)

Omar Khayyám: a rubái = a question.

When Marie Laurencin complained about her back in Henri Rousseau's painting *The Muse Inspiring the Poet* (1909), the Douanier replied: "Guillaume [Apollinaire, Laurencin's lover] is a great poet. He needs a fat muse."

Asked why so many vocal pieces had so much word repetition, the Argentine composer Mauricio Kagel replied, "So that you will start listening to the music."

"You play Bach your way, I'll play him his way."
—Wanda Landowska to a rival

"You have delighted us long enough."
—Mr. Bennet, to his daughter Mary,
playing the pianoforte at a social gathering,
in Jane Austen's *Pride and Prejudice*

"Part needle, part thread."
—a British critic on Beverly Sills's voice,
late in her career

"What is patriotism but the love of the good things we
ate in our childhood?"   —Lin Yutang

"The discovery of a new dish does more for human
happiness than the discovery of a new star."
—Jean Anthelme Brillat-Savarin,
Physiologie du Gout, 1825

"Where is your Self to be found? Always in the deepest enchantment that you have experienced."
—Hugo von Hofmannsthal

"I write for myself in multiplicate."
                                        —Vladimir Nabokov

From Edmond De Goncocurt's *Journal*:

"Taine has the admirable ability to teach others today what he did not know himself yesterday."

"Sickness sensitizes man for observation, like a photographic plate."

"A book is never a masterpiece: it becomes one. Genius is the talent of a dead man."

"Maupassant's books are readable but not re-readable."

"For long, long years I sang songs. When I would sing of love, it turned to pain. And again, when I would sing of pain, it turned to love."(Lieder sang ich nun lange, lange Jahre. Wollte ich Liebe singen, ward zie mir zum Schmerz. Und wollte ich wieder Schmerz nur singen, ward er mir zur Liebe.)
                                        —Franz Schubert, "My Dream"

"Anemones should play the same role in a picture as confidants do in tragedies."   —Ingres

—pinking shear
—a top-dressing of —

"Try to be precise and you are bound to be metaphor-
ical."   —John Middleton Murray

Little Richard:
"Awop-Bop-a-Loo-Mop-Alop-Bam-Boom"

"The Baring family coined the phrase 'Shelley plain'
to mean a personal glimpse of a great man—from
Browning's
          And did you once see Shelley plain,
          And did he stop and speak with you?
In Philip Roth's superb novel *The Professor of Desire* the
professor visits Prague and is taken to meet the aged
whore once fucked by Kafka. She had had a 'Shelley
plain' and would for a consideration reveal to visiting
scholars its central location. To have gone down on
W. H. Auden is a lesser 'Shelley plain,' not so exclu-
sive perhaps, but it's interesting that so many of those
who had the experience are still reluctant to admit it.
It's a narrow niche, one must admit, but still fame of a
sort."   —Alan Bennett

"When we think of forms, they come alive on paper or canvas without having any relation to the forms of life. To be sensitive to the truth of these forms is to understand art. Understanding life is something else entirely."
—Jean Cocteau

"Fame: I picture a bust with legs for running around everywhere."
—Jean Cocteau

"If someone asks me, 'What did you eat?' and I make a mistake in my answer, I will rectify it the next day even if I'm taken for mad, for I believe that exactitude, even in trifles [même dans le menu], is the basis of all greatness."
—Jean Cocteau (advice to the poet)

"My advice to a budding literary critic would be as follows. Learn to distinguish banality. Remember that mediocrity thrives on 'ideas.' Beware of the modish message. Ask yourself if the symbol you have detected is not your own footprint. Ignore allegories. By all means place the 'how' above the 'what' but do not let it be confused with the 'so what.' Do not drag in Freud at this point. All the rest depends on personal talent."
—Vladimir Nabokov
(interview in *Wisconsin Studies in Contemporary Literature*, vol. VIII, no. 2, spring 1967)

—bondieuserie

The measure of a poem's "immortality" is the later life it has in other poems. Imitation, appropriation—dismemberment and regeneration—by new poets give the old poem its purchase on life.

"He who would not be frustrate of his hope to write well hereafter in laudable things, ought him selfe to bee a true Poem, that is, a composition and patterne of the best and honourablest things; not presuming to sing high praises of heroic men or famous cities unless he have in himself the experience and practice of all that which is praiseworthy."

—the young John Milton
("An Apology for Smectymnuus," 1642)

"The friends that have it I do wrong
Whenever I remake a song,
Should know what issue is at stake:
It is myself that I remake."   —W. B. Yeats

"Though there is none of it writ as yet, what I look upon as more than half the work is already done, for 'tis all exactly planned."   —Alexander Pope, on his *Brutus* (of which an outline and eight lines remain)

Poetry makes nothing happen? It makes new poems happen. [make = force; happen = chance]

At Maria Callas's Juilliard master classes, a student mezzo muffed the top note of Azucena's "Condotta ell'era in ceppi," and defended herself by insisting the note was "a cry of despair." "It's not a cry of despair," Callas snapped. "It's a B-flat."

Certain poems: overhauled prose.

"Tradition is the living faith of the dead, traditionalism is the dead faith of the living." —Jaroslav Pelikan

"I think I write in order to discover on my shelf a new book which I would enjoy reading, or see a new play that would engross me. That is why the first months of work on a new project are so delightful: you see the book already bound, or the play already produced, and you have the illusion that you will read or see it as though it were a work by another that will give you pleasure."   —Thornton Wilder

"I like writing with a Peacock's Quill; because its Feathers are all Eyes."   —Thomas Fuller

Valéry said that poetry is a language within a language.

"Nature is garrulous to the point of confusion; let the artist be truly taciturn."   —Paul Klee, his diary, 1909

"I have played with quite a few musicians who weren't so good. But as long as they could hold their instruments *correct*, and display their *willingness* to play as *best* they could, I would look over their shoulders and see *Joe Oliver* and several other great masters from my home town. So I shall now close and be just like the little boy who sat on a *block* of *ice*—
           "*My Tale is Told*.
                         "Tell all the Fans
And *All* Musicians, I love Em Madly.
                         Swiss Krissly Yours
                         Louis Armstrong
                         Satchmo"
                                   [handwritten note]

"The closer the look one takes at a word, the greater

the distance from which it looks back."   —Karl Kraus

∞

"They send me all their productions. They think I ap-
prove what they write. But it isn't art."
                    —Sigmund Freud, on the surrealists
                    (from the journal of Princess Marie Bonaparte)

∞

Shaw said that forcible utterance was the great secret
of criticism.

∞

A. C. Benson's requirements for a don's tailoring: the
fashion before last.

∞

"*Apollo* I look back on as the turning point of my life.
In its discipline and restraint, in its sustained one-
ness of tone and feeling, the score was a revelation. It
seemed to tell me that I could dare not to use everything; that I, too, could eliminate."
                    —George Balanchine

∞

"An old story goes that Cimabue was struck with
admiration when he saw the shepherd boy, Giotto,
sketching sheep. But according to the true biographies, it is never the sheep that inspire a Giotto with
the love of painting: but, rather, his first sight of the

paintings of such a man as Cimabue. What makes the artist is the circumstance that in his youth he was more deeply moved by the sight of works of art than by that of the things which they portray."

—André Malraux, *Psychology of Art*

". . . an ideology expresses secondary and derivative human concerns, and what ideologies are derived from is mythology, which expresses the primary desires of existence, along with the anxieties attached to their frustration. The real object of deconstruction, then, is to reveal the mythological basis under the ideology, and the writers least in need of such analysis are the great reshapers of myth, of whom Rousseau is obviously one. . . . I introduce the point because ideology is always nostalgic for the past or expectant of the future, or both, whereas mythology transposes everything with a present directly confronting the reader." —Northrop Frye, from a review of Paul de Man's *The Rhetoric of Romanticism* (in the January 17, 1986 issue of the *Times Literary Supplement*)

amuse-gueules — the short introductory poem(s) in a volume?

"Poets obey the same laws as summer resorts. The fashion moves continuously in the direction of the

less well known and away from the popular, which have to be rediscovered for different reasons."
—Cyril Connolly, 1967 review of Basil Bunting
in *The Evening Colonnade*, page 362

"If you paint the leaf on a tree without using a model you risk becoming stereotyped, because your imagination will only supply you with a few leaves whereas Nature offers you millions, all on the same tree. No two leaves are exactly the same. The artist who paints only what is in his mind must very soon repeat himself."   —Pierre Renoir, quoted by Jean Renoir in his
1974 autobiography, *My Life and My Films*

Les chiens sont fidèles, mais pas aux chiennes.
[Male dogs are faithful but not to female dogs.]

"Lust is a spirit, which whoso'er doth raise,
The next man that encounters boldly, lays."
—Tourneur

"I read like a laboratory frog with an electrode in its leg."   —Marianne Moore on her reading style

"I must—like a gibbon in a tornado—subdue my chaos. I work at six things at once and will not let one

clipping be disturbed lest my whole Soviet Union fall
to pieces."   —Marianne Moore

"Edith Sitwell, dying, said there was one thing she
regretted: she had never done that thing that they talk
about."   —Robert Duncan, in an essay about H.D.

The "personal" does not lie behind but upon a work
of art: not Turner lashed to the mast in order to experience the storm at sea he will translate into a chaos
of colors, but his fingerprint still visible today in the
glob of pigment applied to make the sun that drove
that storm aside.

"La récompense des grands hommes, c'est que, long-
temps après leur mort, on n'est pas bien sûr qu'ils
sont morts." [The reward for great men is that, for a
long time after they die, one isn't quite sure they are
dead.]   —Jules Renard, *Journals*

"If you never look just wrong to your contemporaries
you will never look just right to posterity—every writer has to be, to some extent, sometimes, a law unto
himself."   —Randall Jarrell, from a review of
                    Richard Wilbur's *Ceremony* (1951)

January 30, 1958

Dear Mr. Jones,

      I thank you for your letter, for
sending me the article written with such care and
sensibility, and for encouraging me about my
translation of the La Fontaine Fables. I am pleased
that you noticed — that you value the phrase, "slaves
whom they themselves have bound." Noone has, so
far as I know, paused upon it.

      I am sorry - very sorry - that you are
menaced by heart attacks.

      It is of much interest to me, what
you say of Christ's thirty-three years as symbolic.
I am indeed very much indebted to you for devoting
effort and thought to me, even at risk to your health.
I hope you will not be penalized for have reason
to regret this effort.

        Sincerely yours,

        Marianne Moore

"To write well, one needs a natural facility and acquired difficulties."   —Jean Jouvet

Friedrich Hebbel:
       "Beauty is the depth of the surface."
       "Beauty: the genius of matter."

Asked by a magazine survey "why do you write?"
Samuel Beckett responded: "Bon qu'à ça." [All I'm
good for.]

Non Multa Sed Multum —Schopenhauer's motto for
his Collected Works

"Singular and Particular Detail is the Foundation of
the Sublime."   —William Blake

—Scrape X off my shoes.
—Gongereauté

"It is never with impunity that one's lips say Love's Litany. Words have their mystical power over the soul, and form can create the feeling from which it should have sprung. Sincerity itself, the ardent, momentary sincerity of the artist, is often the unconscious result of style . . ." —Oscar Wilde, "The Portrait of Mr. W. H."

Evelyn Waugh described the game pie served by Lord Berners's cook as "quite black inside and full of beaks and shot and inexplicable vertebrae."

The saber-sharp critic and poet Clive James reports that his fellow Australian poet Peter Porter said that Auden didn't love God, he just found Him attractive.

"Un poème doit être une fête de l'Intellect."
[A poem ought to be a feast of the Intellect.]
                                   —Paul Valéry, "Litterature"

"It is important for us to realize that many of the qualities of good poetry are irreconcilable."
                                   —Randall Jarrell

"The poetic imagination is seldom able either to overcome or to absorb the devices by which alone it undertakes its greater reaches."   —R. P. Blackmur,
                    "The Shorter Poems of Thomas Hardy"

"Half our sleeping knowledge is in nonsense; and when put in a poem it wakes."   —R. P. Blackmur,
                    "Examples of Wallace Stevens"

". . . a really great artist can never judge of other people's work at all, and can hardly, in fact, judge of his own . . . The gods are hidden from each other. They can recognize their worshippers. That is all."
                    —Oscar Wilde, *The Artist as Critic*

—using X to jump-start the poem

The Cherokee, seeing for the first time the white man's magic of writing, called written documents "talking leaves."

"To criticize is to appreciate, to appropriate, to take

intellectual possession, to establish in fine a relation
with the criticized thing and make it one's own."

—Henry James,
Preface to *What Maisie Knew* (New York Edition)

"You think I know fuck nothing, when in fact I know
fuck all!"   —Ernest Ansermet, who prided himself
on his command of English idioms,
to a British orchestra during a rehearsal

"Young painters do not need criticism. What they
need is praise. They know well enough what is wrong
with their work. What they don't know is what is right
with it."   —Gertrude Stein

"I am I because my little dog knows me."
—Gertrude Stein

"All literature is to me me."
—Gertrude Stein, in a letter to Edmund Wilson

François Bouchet is reported to have said that he did
not paint from life because nature is "too green and
badly lit."

"Il faut choisir: une chose ne peut pas être à la fois vraie et vraisembable." [One has to choose: a thing cannot be at once true and lifelike.]

—Georges Braque

∞

"We should be so much in favor of tragedy and irony as not to think it good policy to require them in all our poems, for fear we might bring them into bad fame."

—John Crowe Ransom

∞

George Orwell on *Ulysses*: "a matter of *daring* just as much as of technique."

∞

"As I can but not as I would."   —Jan Van Eyck's motto

∞

Goldwynisms:

"For your information, I'd like to ask you a question."

"When I want your opinion I'll give it to you."

"I'm exhausted from not talking."

"You and I have a big problem. You've got Gary Cooper, and I want him." (to rival producer Adolf Zucker)

Arthur C. Danto would define sculpture as the embodiment in a material object of the artist's interpretation of it.

On the overemphasis of clarity in writing: A. J. Liebling said the only way to make clear pea soup is to leave out the peas.

"I keep making mistakes, like God." —Pablo Picasso

"To be idle requires a strong sense of personal identity."   —remark by Robert Louis Stevenson, typed on a card taped on Joyce Carol Oates's office door at Princeton

"This is the best of me; for the rest, I ate, I drank, I slept, I loved, I hated as another. My life was a vapor and is not, but this is what I saw and know. This, if anything of mine, is worth your memory."
    —written by Edward Elgar (quoting John Ruskin) at the end of the score of *Gerontius*

From Jean Cocteau's *Journals*:

On Proust:

Rereading Proust, his snobbery irritates, even when he is making fun of society people. He only makes fun of them as unworthy of the names they bear. He saves everything by the inspired way in which he tells his story. In the same way, his homosexuality is vexing. At the hotel in Balbec, the grooms seem to occupy him more than the famous and bizarre jeunes filles en fleurs.

The more I think about it, the more I suspect that Proust, who studies society the way Fabre studied insects, is entitled to his mistakes about their extremely and ancestrally complicated behavior. What is funny is the adherence he demands of the insects, as when he begged me to persuade Mme de Chavigné to read his books—which comes down to Fabre's demanding that the insects read his. 'Marcel is very sweet'—my neighbor Mme de Chavigné would say to me—'if only he didn't pester us so with his scribbling. I never understand a word of it all—it gives me a headache. He should be satisfied with being amusing.'

Let's be fair. Proust never hesitates to judge society people and accuse them of stupidity. He finds them stupid but superior, which is the real basis of snobbery.

Poor, poor Marcel. Poor sick man with his lunatic gaze. He knew nothing of love, only the obsessive torments of his lies and his jealousy.

On André Gide:

Will the monstrous stupidity of Gide's *Journal* ever be discovered? What a mountain of hypocrisy and lies concealed by the pretense of telling the truth limited to the picturesque.

Of course, it's not because he speaks ill of me and lies about me that I find Gide's *Journal* ridiculous. It is the dreariest herbarium, that *Journal*, the most trivial collection of dried plants, for all the Latin labels. I've met Protestant pastors in Switzerland who spend their vacations on such tasks: filling herbariums with perfectly familiar plants and labeling them with unknown names."

"Treason is a matter of dates."   —Talleyrand

The famous archeologist Arthur Evans said the only sport he was good at was jumping to conclusions.

"In literature, as in love, we are astonished at what is chosen by others."   —André Maurois

"Never lend books, for no one ever returns them; the

only books I have in my library are books that other folks have lent me."   —Anatole France

※

"A book is a mirror; if an ass peers into it, you can't expect an apostle to peer out."
—Georg Christoph Lichtenberg

※

"I suggest that the only books that influence us are those for which we are ready, and which have gone a little farther down our particular path than we have yet gone ourselves."   —E. M. Forster

※

"Poetry is not conversation, and I see no reason why poetry should be called upon to imitate conversation. Conversation is the most careless and formless of human utterance; it is spontaneous and unrevised, and its vocabulary is commonly limited. Poetry is the most difficult form of human utterance; we revise poems carefully in order to make them more nearly perfect. The two forms of expression are extremes, they are not close to each other. We do not praise a violinist for playing as if he were improvising; we praise him for playing well. And when a man plays well or writes well, his audience must have intelligence, training, and patience in order to appreciate him. We do not understand difficult matters 'naturally.' "   —Yvor Winters, "Robert Frost; or, the Spiritual Drifter as Poet" (1957)

Philip Roth, from an interview in *The London Review of Books* (5 March 1987):

"I don't think any more about them [his "audience"] when I'm at work than they think of me when they're at work. They're as remote as the onlookers are to a chess-player concentrating on the board and his opponent's game—I feel no more deprived or lonely than he does because people aren't lined up around the block to discuss his every move."

"Novels do influence action, shape opinion, alter conduct—a book can, of course, change somebody's life—but that's because of a choice made by the reader to use the fiction for purposes of his own (purposes that might appall the novelist) and not because the novel is incomplete without the reader taking action. . . . Everything changes everything—nobody argues with that. My point is that whatever changes fiction may appear to inspire have usually to do with the agenda of the reader and not the writer."

"Obsessional themes evolve from astonishment as much as from enduring grievance—a writer is not so much beset by the theme as by his underlying naïveté in the face of it."

Proust, Kafka, Beckett prompt knowledge, not action. They give us a new way of "knowing" the world.

∞

The soprano Elizabeth Söderström told this story about critics: A critic is walking along the seashore, and spies a ship—from which a man suddenly leaps and walks across the water toward him. "Aha," is the critic's reaction, "the man can't swim."

∞

Society doesn't want victims, it wants heroes. But it needs victims so that there may be heroes.

∞

Asked "If your house were burning down and you could take away just one thing, what would it be?" Cocteau replied: "J'emporterai le feu" [I would take the fire].

∞

"But I like the picture of the Flood
and the little babies getting drowned . . .
If I were there I would save them,
but as I can't save them
I like to watch them
getting drowned."   —Lola Ridge, "The Alley"
                                        from *Sun-Up and Other Poems*, 1920

"Elegy is the form of poetry natural to the reflective mind."   —Samuel Taylor Coleridge,
Table Talk, October 23, 1833

"Solipsism coincides with pure realism."
—Ludwig Wittgenstein,
Tractatus Logico-Philosophicus (1922)

"There are ways of getting absolved for murder; there are no ways of getting absolved for upsetting the soup."   —G. K. Chesterton, *Charles Dickens* (1906)

"Great art is the art of simplified figures and of the most pure types; of essences which permit the symmetrical and almost musical development of the consequences from a carefully isolated situation."
—Paul Valéry

Happiness is what I most know of life, but grief is what I best understand of it.

"The verse that is too easie is like the tale of a rosted horse."   —George Gascoigne

"Every morning I read the obituaries in *The Times*.
If I'm not there, I carry on."   —aged English actor
A. E. Mathews (1869-1960), on being asked
when he would cease to hobble the boards

"Does it not occur to these people that I may be artificial by nature?"   —Maurice Ravel, on his critics

". . . for whom nature had refined on the impossible
by relieving them of the sense of the difficult."
—Henry James, "The Tree of Knowledge"

Horace: *limae labor* — "the work of the file"

"I just try to put the thing out there and hope somebody will read it. Someone says: 'Whom do you write
for?' I reply: 'Do you read me?' If they say 'Yes,' I say,
'Do you like it?' If they say 'No,' then I say, 'I don't
write for you.'"   —W. H Auden

"This situation of not having a very large audience
has something good in it too. I mean that it educates

you in a certain way: not to consider that great audiences are the most important reward on this earth. I consider that even if I have three people who read me, I mean really read me, it is enough. That reminds me of a conversation I had once upon a time during the only glimpse I ever had of Henri Michaux. It was when he had a stop-over in Athens, coming from Egypt, I think. He came ashore while his ship was in Piraeus just in order to have a look at the Acropolis. And he told me on that occasion: 'You know, my dear, a man who has only one reader is not a writer. A man who has two readers is not a writer either. But a man who has *three* readers (and he pronounced "three readers" as though they were three million), that man is *really* a writer.'"   —George Seferis

"Castle drank two cups of coffee and read *The Times*. He valued the air of respectability that paper always seemed to lend the reader. He saw the man tying up his shoelace fifty yards down the road, and he experienced a similar sense of security to that which he had once felt while he was being carried from his ward in a hospital toward a major operation—he found himself again an object on a conveyor belt which moved him to a destined end with no responsibility, to anyone or anything, even to his own body. Everything would be looked after for better or worse by somebody else. Somebody with the highest professional qualifications. That was the way death ought to come in the end, he thought, as he moved slowly and happily in the wake of the stranger. He always hoped that he would move toward death with the same sense that

before long he would be released from anxiety forever."   —Graham Greene, *The Human Factor*

"Cinema is simply pieces of film put together in a
manner that creates ideas and emotions."
                              —Alfred Hitchcock

"The middle way . . . is the only road that does not
lead to Rome."   —Arnold Schoenberg,
                              foreword to *Drei Satiren*

Fredric Jameson: "the waning of affect" is a sign of
the cultural times.

"My favorite prose sentence by Mr. Ezra Pound is in
one of his published letters: 'All the Jew part of the
Bible is black evil.' And they ask me to take that seri-
ously as a Western mind."   —Harold Bloom, from an
interview by Imre Salusinszky in *Criticism in Society*

"Even their tender poems have sad subjects."
                              —Goethe, on English poets

"What constitutes adultery is not the hour which a
woman gives her lover, but the night which she after-

wards spends with her husband."   —George Sand

_∞

"Rome, Italy, is an example of what happens when the buildings in a city last too long."   —Andy Warhol, *The Philosophy of Andy Warhol* (1975)

_∞

"Voltaire has said many new things and many true things, but the new ones are not true and the true ones are not new."   —Gotthold Ephraim Lessing

_∞

"The only thing one can be proud of is of having worked in such a way that an official reward for your labor cannot be envisaged by anyone." —Jean Cocteau

_∞

Rossini might interpolate *arie del sorbetto* (while the audience took a little refreshment) and *arie di baule* ("suitcase arias"—to be taken out as needed to fill unexpected gaps).

_∞

Oscar Wilde:

"Poets know how useful passion is for publication. Nowadays a broken heart will run to many editions."

"The well-bred contradict other people. The wise contradict themselves."

"Only the shallow know themselves."

"A truth ceases to be true when more than one person believes in it."

☒

"In those days I seemed to have had two muses: the essential, hysterical, genuine one, who tortured me with elusive snatches of imagery and wrung her hands over my inability to appropriate the magic and madness offered me; and her apprentice, her palette girl and stand-in, a little logician, who stuffed the torn gaps left by her mistress with explanatory or meter-mending fillers which became more and more numerous the further I moved away from the initial, evanescent, savage perfection."
—Vladimir Nabokov, *Look at the Harlequins* (1974)

∞

"Audiences don't like plays where people write letters with feathers."   —Lee Shubert

☒

"One hates an author that's all author."
                         —Lord Byron, *Beppo*

☒

—of a high denomination.

∞

"I know nothing that contributes more to a clear insight into the true nature of any literary phenomenon, than the comparison of it with some elder production, the likeness of which is striking, yet only apparent, while the difference is real."

—Samuel Taylor Coleridge,
Critique of Bertram, *Biographia Literaria*

∞

What Dr. Johnson calls "temporary poems."

∞

"A poem begins as a lump in the throat, a homesickness, a lovesickness. It finds the thought and the thought finds the words." —Robert Frost

∞

Gerard Manley Hopkins to Coventry Patmore, criticizing him and others for the sloppiness of late Victorian prose—"the strain of address."

∞

"I have a commonplace book for facts and another for poetry, but I find it difficult always to preserve the vague distinction that I had in mind, for the most

beautiful and difficult facts are so much the more poetry and that is their success."
    —Henry David Thoreau, *Journals*, February 18, 1852

"Tu nihil in magno doctus reprehendis Homero?"
[As a scholar, do you find nothing to cavil at in great
Homer?]   —Horace, *Satires*, I.10

"Complexe mais pas compliqué."
[Complex but not complicated.]
                              —Maurice Ravel's motto

"He can take liberties I would not allow myself, because he's less of a musician than I am."
                              —Maurice Ravel

"Sincerity is barely an explanation: it is never an
excuse."   —Remy de Gourmont

"Inspiration is merely the reward for working every
day."   —Charles Baudelaire

"Knowledge not purchased by the loss of power!"
                —Wordsworth, *The Prelude*, Book V

"I cannot believe that any artist can be good who is not more than a bit of a reporting journalist."

—W. H. Auden

"Quantity of pleasure being equal, push-pin is as good as poetry."   —Misquote/paraphase by John Stuart Mill of Jeremy Bentham, *The Rationale of Reward* (1811, first published in English in 1825)

Tennyson, *In Memoriam*:

"When Time hath sunder'd shell from pearl" (LII)

"Short swallow-flights of song, that dip
Their wings in tears, and shine away." (XLVIII)

—*tragedie larmoyante*

Destitutus ventis, remos adhibere [If there is no wind, row]   —Latin adage

"One of the disadvantages of wine is that it makes a man mistake words for thoughts."   —Dr. Johnson

"When I described how Emma Bovary poisoned herself, I had such a strong taste of arsenic in my mouth, I was so poisoned myself, that I had two attacks of indigestion, one after the other, very real attacks, for I vomited my entire dinner."   —Gustave Flaubert

"No passion in the world is equal to the passion to alter someone else's draft."   —H. G. Wells

"It's a short walk from the hallelujah to the hoot."
—Nabokov

Nietzsche held the "refinement of cruelty belongs to the springs of art."

Thomas Campion spoke of poems that "warmed themselves at fantastical fires and danced in the light of glowworms."

"Browning has, I think, many frigidities. Any untruth to nature, to human nature, is frigid. Now he has got a great deal of what came in with Kingsley and the Broad Church School, a way of talking (and making his people talk) with the air and spirit of a man bouncing up from the table with a mouth full of bread and cheese and saying that he meant to stand no blasted nonsense."   —Gerard Manley Hopkins, in a 12 October 1881 letter to Canon Richard Watson Dixon

"Fashion dies very young, so we must forgive it everything."   —Jean Cocteau

A rival designer on the Chanel look (supposedly based on "the simple dress of the working girl"): "deluxe poverty"

In "At Galway Races" (1916), Yeats refers to "hearers and hearteners of the work."

". . . we reflect in general not to find the facts, but to prove our theories at the expense of them."
—F. H. Bradley,
in "The Vulgar Notion of Responsibility in Connection with the Theories of Free Will and Necessity"

Tom Paulin uses the Irish word *thrawn* to refer to a poetry or language where there's "something a bit difficult, a bit contorted," as in Donne or Hopkins or Browning (or Frost, he adds, and Hardy).

∞

Thomas Hobbes described wit as the "swift succession of one thought to another, and steady direction to some approved end."

∞

For the Greeks, memory was "the water of longing."

∞

—A critic named Hughschall B. Nameless (Hugh Shelby-Nameless).

∞

Asked on a visit to London what he thought of Western civilization, Mahatma Gandhi replied that he thought it would be a very good idea.

∞

"This is what a picture should give us . . . an abyss in which the eye is lost, a secret germination, a colored state of grace . . . Lose consciousness. Descend with the painter into the dim tangled roots of things, and rise again from them in colors, be steeped in the light of them."   —Paul Cézanne, apparently commenting on Veronese's *The Marriage Feast at Cana*

"But even as one searches for a way to express what one senses as a limitation, one remembers this poet's youth and remembers also that it was precisely those intense personal needs which gave her work its unprecedented pitch and scald. Her poems already belong to the tradition not just because they fulfill the poetic needs I outlined at the beginning—but because they are also clearly acts of her being, words from which, in Buber's terms, effective power streams. They demonstrate the truth of Wordsworth's wonderful formulation, in his 1802 preface to Lyrical Ballads, of the way poetic knowledge gets expressed. Wordsworth's account is the finest I know of the problematic relation between artistic excellence and truth, between Ariel and Prospero, between poetry as impulse and poetry as criticism of life. The following quotation includes a perhaps over-familiar sentence, and may show some syntactical strain, but it covers a lot of the essential ground:

" 'Now that I mean to say, that I always began to write with a distinct purpose formally conceived; but I believe that my habits of meditation have so formed my feelings, as that my description of such objects excite those feelings, will be found to carry along with them a purpose. If in this opinion I am mistaken, I can have little right to the name of a poet. For all good poetry is the spontaneous overflow of powerful feelings: but though this be true, poems to which any value can be attached, were never produced on any variety of subjects but by a man, who being possessed of more than usual organic sensibility, had also thought long and deeply. For our continued influxes of feeling are modified and directed by our thoughts, which are indeed the representation of all our past feelings; and, as by contemplating the relations of these general representatives to each other we discover what is really important to men, so by the repetition and continuance of this act, our feelings will be connected with important subjects, till at length, if we be originally possessed of much sensibility, such habits of mind will be produced, that, by obeying blindly and mechanically the impulses of those habits, we shall describe objects, and utter sentiments of such a nature and in such connection with each other, that the understanding of the being to whom we address ourselves, if he be in a healthful state of association, must necessarily be in some degree enlightened, and his affections ameliorated.'

"Essentially, Wordsworth declares that what counts is the quality, intensity and breadth of the poet's concerns between the moments of writing, the gravity and purity of the mind's appetites and applications between moments of inspiration. This is what determines the ultimate human value of the act of poetry. That act remains free, self-governing, self-seeking, but the worth of the booty it brings back from its raid upon the inarticulate will depend upon the emotional capacity, intellectual resource and general civilization which the articulate poet maintains between the raids."   —Seamus Heaney, on Sylvia Plath

"The natural enemy of any subject is the professor thereof."   —William James

Memory is a beloved old neighborhood. In time, the wrong sort of people start moving in.

Eadweard Muybridge's sequential photographs — Egyptian hieroglyphics.

"The Nazis were criminals. Imagine, they closed the theaters and my operas could not be given!"
                                                    —Richard Strauss

"How well they go together, bad taste and vigor."
                    —Igor Stravinsky on *Der Rosenkavalier*

"To look means to forget the names of the things one is seeing."   —Paul Valéry, on Degas

The change in Kavanaugh reminds Heaney of his changing sense of a chestnut that one of his aunts planted the year he was born. As the chestnut grew to a tree in her garden, he came to identify his life with it. But after the family moved, the tree was cut down:

"Then, all of a sudden, a couple of years ago, I began to think of the space where the tree had been or would have been. In my mind's eye I saw it as a kind of luminous emptiness, a warp and waver of light, and once again, in a way that I find hard to define, I began to identify with that space just as years before I had identified with the young tree. Except that this time it was not so much a matter of attaching oneself to a living symbol of being rooted in the native ground; it was more a matter of preparing to be unrooted, to be spirited away into some transparent yet indigenous afterlife. The new place was all idea, if you like. . . . It was and remains an imagined realm . . . a placeless heaven rather than a heavenly place."
                    —Seamus Heaney, "The Placeless Heaven:
                              Another Look at Kavanaugh"

"Missing the pillow that was supposed to cushion his stinging blows, John Hargreaves hit Wendy Hughes, his co-star in 'My First Wife,' just below the ear.

" 'She instantly hated me and started spitting venom,' recalled Mr. Hargreaves, who dated Miss Hughes after they attended drama school together about 20 years ago. 'It wasn't a character hitting back. It wasn't acting. It was us. She hated me.'

" 'I got really upset,' the 33-year-old Miss Hughes said. 'Tears were rolling down my cheek. It hurt. I was so angry. I wanted to hit back. It wasn't the character. It was real. It was me.'

"Both Mr. Hargreaves and Miss Hughes said that when they had finished the scene, they thought they had transcended their characters, fused their roles and their lives into a near perfect performance. But the director, Paul Cox, felt it was flawed. He said he had a 'hunch' that they could do better. Overriding their quarrelsome protests, he insisted that they re-shoot the scene.

" 'We felt mechanical the second time,' Mr. Hargreaves recalled. 'It felt tinny. We thought the first time was infinitely better, infinitely more real.' But when the two takes were printed and compared, both actors agreed with Mr. Cox: the emotions released by the errant blow in the first take had assumed a life of their own. They had overwhelmed the characters. Falling out of character, Miss Hughes and Mr. Hargreaves had responded to the pent-up pain and, like most hurt people, had run.

" 'I hid my face the entire time because it was Wendy crying,' Miss Hughes, a one-woman encounter group when performing, said in a recent interview in New York. 'The second time it was in character and I played it to the camera. It was better.'

" 'Because it was real, we were hiding it,' Mr. Hargreaves added in a telephone interview from Australia. "The real emotions got in the way. They were too much.' "   —from a newspaper piece (28 April 1985) about the 1984 Australian film *My First Wife*

His ideas seem to have been lifted from fortune cookies.

In Dutch still lifes, the multiplying white dots both represent gleams of light and create them.

"There is no longer a virtuous nation, and the best of us live by candlelight."   —W. B. Yeats, in a letter

The notion, or metaphor, of the literary banquet — such as concocted by Erasmus, Giordano Bruno, Béroalde de Verville, or Rabelais.

"Criticism is prejudice made plausible."
                              —H. L. Mencken

"Those who have free seats boo first."
                              —Chinese saying

"When you start working, everybody is in your studio—the past, your friends, enemies, the art world, and above all, your own ideas—all are there. But as you continue, they start leaving one by one, and you are left completely alone. Then, if you're lucky, even you leave." —John Cage to Philip Guston in the 1950s

"It is hard to read a contemporary poet critically; for we go within the shallowest verse and inform it with all the life and promise of this day. We are such a near and kind and knowing audience as he will never have again. We go within the fane of the temple and hear the faint music of worshippers; but posterity will have to stand without and consider the vast proportions and grandeur of the building."
—Henry David Thoreau, *Journal*, October 12, 1842

An example of literalism. When Lord Cornbury opened the New York Assembly in 1702 in drag—in the style of Queen Anne, in fact—and was challenged, he is reported to have answered: "You are all very stupid people not to see the propriety of it all. In this place, and on this occasion, I represent a woman, and in all respects I ought to represent her as faithfully as I can."

" 'I distinguish the picturesque and the beautiful, and I add to them, in the laying out of grounds, a third and distinct character, which I call unexpectedness.'

" 'Pray, sir,' said Mr. Milestone, 'by what name do you distinguish this character, when a person walks round the grounds for the second time?' "
—Thomas Love Peacock, *Headlong Hall* (1816)

—his squeeze-box
—but less of that anon

"For the last third of life there remains only work. It alone is always stimulating, rejuvenating, exciting and satisfying."　　　　　　　—Käthe Kollwitz

"When the axe came into the forest, the trees said the handle is one of us."　　　　—Turkish proverb

Apropos the work of other artists becoming more spare, it should be noted that this is not always obvious; *Parsifal* is the thinnest of Richard Wagner's scores (in terms of printed bulk).

"To give an accurate and exhaustive account of that period would need a far less brilliant pen than mine."
—Max Beerbohm

"When I was four, I could draw as well as Raphael. It has taken me my whole life to learn to draw like a child."
—Picasso

Rossini: "La Musique Anodine."

From Cesare Pavese's diary:

"Great modern art is always ironic, just as ancient art was religious. In the same way that a sense of the sacred was rooted in visions beyond the world of reality, giving them backgrounds and antecedents pregnant with significance, so irony discovers, beneath and within such visions, a vast field for intellectual sport, a vibrant atmosphere of imaginative and closely reasoned methods of treatment that make the things that are represented into symbols of a more significant reality. . . . It is enough to create imaginative visions according to a standard that transcends or governs them." (22 February 1942)

"If it is true that a man marries, for preference, his opposite (the 'law of life'), that is because we have an instinctive horror of being tied to someone who displays the same defects and idiosyncrasies as ourselves. The reason is obviously that defects and idiosyncrasies, discovered in someone near to us, rob us of the illusion—which we formerly fostered—that in ourselves they would be eccentricities, excusable because of their originality." (20 May 1940)

"Remember, writing poetry is like making love: one will never know whether one's own pleasure is shared." (17 November 1937)

"The greatest benefit that a writer brings to poetry, to literature, is that part of his life which, while living it, seemed to him the furthest removed from literature." (12 May 1947)

"Writing is a fine thing, because it combines the two pleasures of talking to yourself and talking to a crowd." (4 May 1946)

"Why do we find any new writer tiresome? Because we do not yet know enough about him to visualize him in a social environment we would feel confident in sharing." (5 November 1939)

"No woman marries for money: they are all clever enough, before marrying a millionaire, to fall in love with him first." (14 April 1941)

"The beautiful girls you will have seen at Nîmes will not, I am certain, delight your spirit less than the sight of the beautiful columns of the Maison Carrée, since the latter are only ancient copies of the former."
—Nicolas Poussin, in a 1642 letter to his friend
Paul Fréart de Chantelou

"Degas, with little tenderness for anybody, was not apt to be indulgent of criticism, or of theories. He was always ready to assert—and later in life he would harp on it—that there is no arguing among the muses. They work all day, very much on their own. In the evening, work finished, they get together and dance; they do not talk."   —Paul Valéry, "Degas Danse Desir"

Told that a certain poem resembled an older poem, Allen Tate replied: "It had damn well better!"

Robert Frost's remark about Edward Arlington Robinson is as well true of his own art: that he was "content with the old-fashion way to be new."

Partir, c'est mourir un peu, mais mourir, c'est partir trop. [To leave is to die a little, but to die is to leave altogether.]

Ernest Hemingway said there are two ways to spend the evening. Get into your Buick, shut the windows, and sit near the exhaust. Or go to a cocktail party.

On a postcard from the old, ailing Auden to composer Robin Holloway who'd asked him for a libretto based on *Miss Lonelyhearts*: "Too sad to sing."

The story is told—I think of Brahms—that the master was made to listen to a new score by a young composer. As he did, he kept raising his hat. The young man asked him why. "I'm just saying hello to old friends," he replied.

"Minds are formed by the character of a language, rather than language being formed by the minds of those who speak it."   —Giambattista Vico

"Physiological life is of course not 'Life.' And neither is psychological life. Life is the world."
                                        —Ludwig Wittgenstein

"Nothing I wrote prevented one Jew from being gassed." —Auden, in a 1971 interview

"Poets are jails. Works are the convicts who escape."
—Jean Cocteau, *Diary*, 23 March 1953

Fernando Pessoa's heteronyms: Álvaro de Campos, Ricardo Reis, Alberto Caeiro

"Dynamite is the least dangerous thing Nobel ever invented." —Paul Morand

"Letters! Everyone wants you to read him, to praise him, to write a preface for him, to influence his publishers. Everyone wants you to make his films, to place his plays. Everyone imagines that fate is against him and that luck is always on your side.

"The older I grow, the more I realize that fame (whatever is called fame) is the consequence of an architectural and geometrical phenomenon hidden under the apparent disorders of nature. It is not our works which get us anywhere. It's a harmony of energies which escape our individual ethic, invisible to everyone. Everyone experiences them, though they oppose them and are utterly unaware of them. This is how a name is formed and becomes powerful outside works that are almost always misunderstood and poorly read. I would have been abandoned long since if my works had to function by themselves."

—Cocteau, Diary, 15 May 1953

"What is called my intelligence is nothing but my capacity to pay attention and a morbid horror of inexactitude."   —Cocteau, *Diary*, 11 June 1953

"Surface excesses have spoiled eyes which recognize a fashion by its costumes and never consult the work's own gaze. Yet it is by the gaze that we recognize new beauty, whatever its costume."

—Cocteau, Diary, 21 June 1953

"One is never understood. One is accepted."

—Eugène Delacroix

Delius called Richard Strauss "the modern Meyerbeer."

Theodore Roethke had submitted "The Lost Son" to *Horizon*. Sonia Brownell (later Orwell) returned it with the remark: "It seemed to us that your poetry was in a way very American in that it just lacked that inspiration, inevitability or quintessence of writing and feeling that distinguishes good poetry from verse."

∞

Kafka wrote his diary all during World War I, and there is not a single reference to the war in all his reflections.

∞

Stravinsky once scolded his son Theodore: "How dare you insult someone so handsome!"

∞

"Drogulus" (coined by A. J. Ayer): "An entity whose presence is unverifiable because it has no physical effects."

∞

Aretino's Postures

∞

Lanami — the season of cherry blossom viewing

∞

"In the end most things in life—perhaps all things— turn out to be appropriate."   —Anthony Powell

∞

To the wounds of his victims, Torquemada applied
thistle poultices.

"Success is a result, not the goal."   —Flaubert

"Exuberance is Beauty."   —Blake

Which Mandarin has the longest fingernails?

"The best cure for loneliness is solitude."
        —Marianne Moore

Inigo Jones wrote in his notebook at Rome in 1614
(act. 41): "Altis diletto che Imparat non trous" [I find
no other pleasure than learning].

"Drawing is not form, it's the way you see form."
        —Degas

Nigel Dennis used to complain about "two-volume biographies of one-volume persons."

"When I am, as it were, completely myself, entirely alone, and of good cheer—say, traveling in a carriage, or walking after a good meal, or during the night when I cannot sleep; it is on such occasions that my ideas flow best and most abundantly. *Whence* and *how* they come, I know not; nor can I force them. Those ideas that please me I retain in memory, and am accustomed, as I have been told, to hum them to myself. If I continue in this way it soon occurs to me how I may turn this or that morsel to account, so as to make a good dish of it, that is to say, one agreeable to the rules of counterpoint, to the peculiarities of various instruments, etc.

"All this fires my soul, and, provided I am not disturbed, my subject enlarges itself, becomes methodized and defined, and the whole, though it be long, stands almost complete and finished in my mind, so that I can survey it, like a fine picture or a beautiful statue, at a glance. . . .

"When I proceed to write down my ideas, I take out of the bag of my memory, if I may use that phrase, what has been previously collected into it in the way I have mentioned. For this reason the committing to paper is done quickly enough, for everything is, as I said before, already finished; and it rarely differs on paper from what it was in my imagination. At this occupation I can therefore suffer myself to be disturbed; for whatever may be going on around me, I write, and even talk but only of fowls and geese, or of Gretel or Barbel, or some such matters. But why my productions take from my hand that particular form and style that makes them *Mozartish*, and different from the works of other composers, is probably owing to the same cause which renders my nose so large and aquiline, or, in short, makes it Mozart's, and different from those of other people. For I really do not study or aim at originality."

—from a (forged) Mozart letter

"Art is not difficult because it wishes to be difficult, rather because it wishes to be art. However much the writer might long to be straightforward, these virtues are no longer available to him. He discovers that in being simple, honest, straightforward, nothing much happens. . . . Writing is a process of dealing with not-knowing, a forcing of what and how."

—Donald Barthelme, quoted by the *Times*
in its obituary of him, 24 July 1989

"Some people think that luxury is the opposite of poverty. Not so. It is the opposite of vulgarity."

—Coco Chanel

"Rem tene, verba sequentur."
[Know your subject, words will follow.]

—Cato the Elder

"Behind each jewel are three thousand sweating horses."
                                                    —Zen saying

"Non satis est pulchra esse poemata."
[It's not enough for poems to be beautiful.]
                                                    —Horace, *Ars Poetica*

"Rien ne dure au monde que le tourment."
[Nothing in this world lasts, grief excepted.]
                                                    —Du Bellay

"J'accepte les régimes, mais pas les manies."
[I'll put up with diets but not manias.]
                                        —the cook in Jean Renoir's *La Règle du jeu*

—bread and circuses.

"Technique in art . . . has about the same value as technique in lovemaking, That is to say, heartfelt ineptitude has its appeal and so does heartless skill, but what you want is passionate virtuosity."

                                                    —John Barth

cf. Hopkins, *Letters*, 171, 174, where he laments that if

his poems are too clear they will be misunderstood.

"Nescit vox missa reverti." [The voice sent forth can
never be recalled.]   —Horace, *Ars Poetica*, 390

"So repulsive in others, in oneself of course the only
dignified thing."   —Cyril Connolly, on failure

"The final skill of a poet lies in his so conducting the
work he does deliberately do, that the other work—the
hidden work, the inspiration, the genius—becomes
increasingly available not only in new poems but in
old poems re-read." —R. P. Blackmur, "The Shorter
Poems of Thomas Hardy" (his example here is Yeats)

". . . in poetry you make judgments by your own preliminary choice of symbols, and force the reader who
accepts the symbols to accept the judgments implicit
in them."   —Randall Jarrell, "Texts from Housman"

"What was life, really? It was warmth, the warmth
produced by instability attempting to preserve form,
a fever of matter that accompanies the ceaseless dis-

solution and renewal of protein molecules, themselves transient in their complex and intricate construction. It was the existence of what, in actuality, has no inherent ability to exist, but only balances with sweet, painful precariousness on one point of existence in the midst of this feverish, interwoven process of decay and repair. It was not matter, it was not spirit. It was something in between the two, a phenomenon borne by matter, like the rainbow above a waterfall, like a flame. But although it was not material, it was sensual to the point of lust and revulsion, it was matter shamelessly sensitive to stimuli within and without—existence in its lewd form. It was a secret, sensate stirring in the chaste chill of space. It was furtive, lascivious, sordid—nourishment sucked in and excreted, an exhalation of carbon dioxide and other foul impurities of a mysterious origin and nature. Out of overcompensation for its own instability, yet governed by its own inherent laws of formation, a bloated concoction of water, protein, salt, and fats— what we call flesh—ran riot, unfolded and took shape, achieving form, ideality, beauty, and yet all the while was the quintessence of sensuality and desire. This form and this beauty were not derived from the spirit, as in works of poetry and music, nor derived from some neutral material both consumed by spirit and innocently embodying it, as is the case with the form and beauty of the visual arts. Rather, they were derived from and perfected by substances awakened to lust via means unknown, by decomposing and composing organic matter itself, by reeking flesh."

—Thomas Mann, *The Magic Mountain*

"Hold on and hold off."   —Stoic motto

"Wagner is the Puccini of music."   —Stravinsky

Virgil Thomson, watching a beautiful woman walk toward him on the street, turned to a companion and whispered, "It's at times like this I wish I were a lesbian."

"Go to the pine if you want to learn about the pine, or to the bamboo if you want to learn about the bamboo. And in doing so, you must let go of your subjective preoccupation with yourself. Your poetry arises by itself when you and the object have become one, when you have plunged deep enough into the object to see something like a hidden light glimmering there. However well phrased your poetry may be, if your feeling isn't natural—if you and the object are separate—then your poetry isn't true poetry but merely your subjective counterfeit."   —Basho (1644-1694)

"Men are admitted into Heaven not because they have curbed and governed their Passions or have No Passions, but because they have Cultivated their Understandings."   —Blake

"Enlightenment is like the moon reflected in the water. The moon doesn't get wet; the water isn't broken. Although its light is wide and vast, the moon is reflected even in a puddle an inch long. The whole moon and the whole sky are reflected in a dewdrop on the grass."   — Kigen Dōgen (1200-1253)

"Maturity—to recover the seriousness one had as a child at play."   —Nietzsche (and a favorite of Auden's)

"Les natures profondément bonnes sont tojours indécises." [Profoundly good natures are always doubtful.]   —Ernest Renan

X's work is like a Grinling Gibbons carving.

"Every writer is a parodist in love with what he mimics."
                                —some critic or other

In his introduction to William Dickey's volume in the Yale Younger Poets series (1959), Auden discusses his criteria for choosing such a book.

About Velásquez's portrait of Juan de Pareja: When Pareja first showed it to some of Velasquez's friends, they were astounded by the likeness, and looking from portrait to model, model to portrait, didn't know which to address or where the response would come from.

A dream last night in which I described myself as a "Greek-Roman husband and wife"—referring either to my inner or my literary life. A point was made. Could the poet in me be the Greek, and the critic the Roman?

"I need more than one factor, [I need] at least two. Two factors that are not related in any way. The creative act for me rests in the coupling of these two different factors in order to produce something new, which might be called a plastic poem."   —Man Ray

Proust on Madame de Guermantes:
She was inclined "to a style of conversation that rejects everything to do with fine language and expression of lofty thoughts, so that she made a sort of point of good breeding when she was with a poet or a musician to talk only of the food that they were

eating or the game of cards to which they would afterwards sit down. This abstention had, on a third
person not conversant with her ways, a disturbing
effect which amounted to mystification. Mme de
Guermantes having asked him if he would like to be
invited to meet this or that famous poet, devoured by
curiosity he would arrive at the appointed hour. The
Duchess would talk to the poet about the weather.
They would sit down to lunch: 'Do you like this way
of doing eggs?' she would ask the poet. On hearing
his approval, which she shared, for everything in her
own house appeared to her exquisite, down to the
horrible cider which she imported from Guermantes: 'give Monsieur some more eggs,' she would tell
the butler, while the anxious fellow-guest sat waiting
for what must surely have been the object of the occasion, since they had arranged to meet, in spite of
every sort of difficulty, before the Duchess, the poet
and he himself left Paris. But the meal went on, one
after another the courses would be cleared away, not
without having provided Mme de Guermantes with
opportunities for clever witticisms or well-judged
anecdotes. Meanwhile the poet would go on eating
without either the Duke or Duchess showing any sign
of remembering that he was a poet. And presently the
luncheon would come to an end and the party would
break up, without a word having been said about
poetry which they nevertheless all admired but to
which, by a reserve analogous to that of which Swann
had given me a foretaste, no one referred. This reserve was simply a matter of good form."

Kleist, from a lecture "Observations on the Way of the World":

"There are people who imagine the eras through which a nation's culture progresses to exist in a quite peculiar order. They imagine that a people starts out down in a state of animal *crudity* and *wildness*; that after a certain period of time they feel the need for an improvement in their morals, and are consequently compelled to draw up the *science of virtue*; that in order to allow access to the theories of that science, the idea arose to symbolize them in beautiful examples, and that in consequence *aesthetics* was invented; and that now, according to the precepts of that science, beautiful symbols were composed, and this gave rise to *art*; and that by means of art the people was finally led to the highest step of human *culture*. These people should be told that everything, at least among the Greeks and the Romans, occurred in an order precisely the reverse of this. These peoples started out with the *heroic* era, beyond a doubt the highest that can be reached; when they no longer had heroes in any human and civic sense, they *wrote* themselves some; when they could no longer write them, they invented the *rules* for doing so; when they got muddled by the rules, they abstracted from them *worldly wisdom* itself; and when they were done with that, they became *bad*."

Poe distinguished between obscurity of expression and the expression of obscurity.

"There must always be enigmas in poetry. That is the aim of literature."   —Mallarmé, 1891

"The *Cantos* refer, but do not present."
                                        —Basil Bunting

On the set of her last film, *The Whales of August*, Bette Davis spent a considerable part of her free time complaining—especially about Joan Crawford. Finally, someone spoke up: "Really, Miss Davis, why *do* you go on about Miss Crawford so. I mean, we all have our faults, and hers are well known. What good does it do to rant on about them. Besides, the woman's been dead for fifteen years!" Bette took a long drag on her cigarette, looked at the young man, and said: "Darling, just because you're dead doesn't mean you've changed."

"Ficta voluptatis causa sint proxima veris." [Fictions meant to please should be close to the truth.]
                                        —Horace

"Parturiunt montes, nascetur mus."
[The mountains labored and delivered a mouse.]
                                —Horace, *Ars Poetica*, 139

"People say life is the thing, but I prefer reading."
                              —Logan Pearsall Smith

Coleridge described himself as a "library-cormorant."

It's mutton dressed as lamb.

As a description of some poetry collection, this old
punch-brewing recipe:
          "One of the sour,
          Two of sweet,
          Four of strong
          And eight of weak."

"Everything that is possible to be believed is an image
of the truth."   —Blake

"Tant pis pour le bois qui se trouve un violon."
[Too bad for the wood that finds itself a violin.]
                              —Rimbaud

Mallarmé said that the French word for "day" sound-
ed like night, and vice versa.

Philip Sidney wanted from poetry a "heart-ravishing knowledge."

"Habent sua fatu libelli." [Books have their desti-nies.]   —Catullus

"Motionless, deep in his mind lies the past the poet's
    forgotten,
Till some small experience wake it to life and a
    poem's begotten,
Words its presumptive primordii, Feeling its field of
    induction,
Meaning its pattern of growth determined during
    construction."
                                    —"New Year Letter"
                        W. H. Auden, note to *The Double Man*

Auden said a poet's prayer is this: "Lord, teach me to write so well, that I shall no longer want to."

"One can only reach out to the universe with a gloved
hand."   —Yeats

Mr. W. H. Auden

requests the pleasure of your company

at

A Birthday Party

on Sunday, February twenty-first

Nineteen hundred and sixty-one

at nine p. m.

R. s. v. p.

77 St. Marks Place

New York City 3 Carriages at one a. m.

"Talk to *me*, Miss West. Don't talk to my husband. He is uneducated, and common."

—Emma Hardy to Rebecca West

—Un mur tilé de guerre
—frog march

"Optima dies prima fugit."   —Virgil

—backbencher
—X got up on his hind legs and . . .
—X is filling a much-needed gap.

"Take back this pudding. It has no theme."

—Winston Churchill

David Hockney reported that in 1973 he had gone to see the portraits of himself with Henry Geldzahler that Andy Warhol had done: "Henry didn't like his— he told Andy that he'd left something out. And Andy said, What? Henry said, You left the art out. And Andy replied, Oh, I knew I forgot something."

"It seems to me that Offenbach's humor, like Mozart's, is poised on the suggestion that false love and true love are not so different as one might wish; they are both of them really tender."   —Edwin Denby

Klimt said to write anything, even a short note, made him "seasick."

"The Way that can be spoken of is not the True Way."
                                                —Lao Tzu

"Whoever undertakes to write a biography binds himself to lying, to concealment, to hypocrisy, to flummery and even to hiding his own lack of understanding."
   —Bruno Bettelheim, quoting Freud on biographers

"Outside of a dog, a book is a man's best friend. Inside of a dog, it's too dark to read."   —Groucho Marx

"No matter what I do, I always wind up on page one."
                                                —Jean Harlow

When Edmund White asked the Duchess of Beaufort what her idea of a nightmare guest is, she replied: "Someone who looks at me full of hope and expectation when I come down in the morning."

Emerson referred to "The Poetry of the Portfolio"— "the work of persons who wrote for relief of their own minds, and without thought of publication."

Trying to persuade Nunnally Johnson to rewrite and direct *Cleopatra* in mid-shoot, the studio asked him to name his price. "Ten percent of the losses," he said.

"I don't mind being listed alphabetically, but I do mind being treated alphabetically."
>   —Maria Tallchief, withdrawing from the
>   New York City Ballet in 1965

"You can't speak too loud or too much in England. If you are awake it's already vulgar."
>   —George Balanchine, on the English

Marianne Moore said she'd made it a principle not to be over-influenced by minor disappointments.

"Warm in bed and drugged to the eyeballs."
    —Kingsley Amis's vision of the moment of death

"This is just the book to give your sister if she's a loud, dirty, boozy girl."   —Dylan Thomas's blurb
                    for Flann O'Brien's *At Swim-Two-Birds*

Ned Rorem once told me that in his eighties he would ask a young man to stand on a chair for a blow-job. He was afraid that, if he knelt, he wouldn't be able to get back on his feet.

On his passport, Stravinsky listed himself as "inventor of sounds."

"Let us then suppose the mind to be, as we say, white Paper, devoid of all Characters, without any *Ideas*: How comes it to be furnished?"   —John Locke

—X is copperbottoming his career
—The Flat Earth Society

Rebecca West labeled Mrs. Humphrey Ward's career "one long specialization in the *mot injuste*."

"Truth is simply a compliment paid to sentences seen to be paying their own way."   —Richard Rorty

When, in her "False Dawn," Edith Wharton writes, "The drawing-room window opened, and from it emerged Mrs. Raycie, in a ruffled sarsnet dress and Point de Paris cap, followed by her two daughters in starched organdy with pink spencers," I can see it all, but have no idea what I am supposed to be looking at.

A feature in today's newspaper describes several drag queens who mount special holiday shows in Manhattan. One opens with "It's Beginning To Look A Lot Like Syphilis."

"The meek are contesting the will."
                              —California bumper sticker

✳

"L'Art est un perpétuel sacrifice de sentiment à la vérité." [Art is the continual sacrifice of feeling to the
truth.]   —Marcel Proust, in a letter, 1919

✳

—sottocapi (Mafia deputies)

✳

"A single strained attitude instead of passion, the
sexless American professor for all his violence."
                    —W. B. Yeats, on Ezra Pound, letter to
                    Dorothy Wellesley, September 8, 1935

"We have all something within ourselves to batten
down and get our power from this fighting."
                    —W.B. Yeats, letter to Dorothy Wellesley,
                                        August 5, 1936

Yeats called Wilfred Owen "unworthy of the poets'
corner of a country newspaper." "He is all blood, dirt
& sucked sugar stick."

"The tragedy of sexual intercourse is the perpetual
virginity of the soul."   —W. B. Yeats

"No artesian well of the intellect can find the poetic
theme."   —W. B. Yeats

"Opera is really the best way of carrying on life. You always sing, and at any crisis you sing a tune—a real tune. And if the crisis is really frightful, you make it the end of the act, pull the curtain down, and have some light refreshment in privacy, and put on another frock."   —E. F. Benson, from *The Angel of Pain*

"Never to lie is to have no lock on your door. You are never alone."   —Elizabeth Bowen

"Ineptitude consists in wanting to reach a conclusion."
                                                  —Flaubert

"One must judge men, not by their opinions, but by what their opinions have made of them."
                                                  —Lichtenberg

"Who plans suicide sitting in the sun?"
                                                  —Elizabeth Smart

"He drafted two Indian boys into his service, one to care for his ass and work in the garden, the other to cook and wait upon him at table."
         —Willa Cather, *Death Comes for the Archbishop*,
                                          Book III, Chapter 4

Boss Tweed said he would rather be a lamppost in New York than the mayor of Philadelphia.

Didactic — *didax*, the teacher's forefinger (a gesture); also dactyl.

"How can I say it? There is a Russian expression that also exists in French. Nabokov offered only two fingers to the world. He did not shake your hand in friendship with all five fingers."

> —Nina Berberova, in an interview,
> explaining why it was better to know Nabokov
> through his writings rather than in person

"For who is there who, shooting all day, will not sometimes hit the mark?"
> —Cicero

Epicurus says that being rich is not an alleviation, but a change, of troubles.

"On ne doit pas la vérité à ses tyrans." [No one owes the truth to tyrants.]
> —Charlotte Corday

"One is not free to write this or that."　　　—Flaubert

"Moods change like the landscapes before a traveler
on a train."　　　　　　　　　　　　　　　—Freud

"Less is not more—less is less!"　　　—Diane Di Vors

For X's work I have not so much an admiration as a
weakness.

"When the best student hears about the Way
He practices it assiduously,
When the average student hears about the Way
It seems to him one moment there and gone the next;
When the worst student hears about the Way
He laughs out loud.
If he did not laugh
It would be unworthy of being the Way."
　　　　　　　　　　　—Lao Tzu, *Tao Te Ching*

"Every true genius must be naïve, or it is not genius."

"The naïve is childlikeness where it is not expected."
—Schiller

A true account of artistic narcissism. A tall, hand-some, talented poet has just given another success-ful, jam-packed reading, and was signing copies of his books at a table. The next person in line was a delicious co-ed, who began gurgling her praise of the poet's work. He paid a blank, polite attention. Then she asked if she could have dinner with him after he finished signing. He didn't even look up from his task, and said he was busy. The girl quickly added that she would give him a blow-job after dinner. The poet hesitated a moment and looked up at her. "Yeah?" he said, "What's in it for me?"

"I probably shan't return before dawn. How I detest the dawn. The grass looks like it's been left out all night."   —Clifton Webb, in *The Dark Corner*

"I don't pray. Kneeling bags my nylons."
—Jan Sterling, in *Ace in the Hole*

"Blow, shyster."   —Robert Ryan, in *The Racket*

Euclid defined the line as breadthless length.

∞

"The minute's extra thought on the choice of a word, or the position of a stress, may make in the lyric a difference of a thousand years."   —Cyril Connolly

∞

"Style never totally beguiles . . . since even when we are so queerly constituted as to be ninety-nine parts literary we are still a hundredth part something else."
        —Henry James, from an essay on Flaubert

∞

"I'm only interested in the *suggestion* of something never seen before."   —Diana Vreeland

∞

Apropos Geraldine Page's "busy" acting style, some director once told her: "Gerry, don't just do something. *Stand* there!"

∞

"Things are more like they are now than they ever were before."   —Eisenhower

∞

"The future is in the laps of the gods, and they're standing up to see what's going to happen."

—proverb

"The young writer is always told (he was, anyhow, when I was young) that writing means first and last 'having something to say.' I cherish as a souvenir of boyhood that honorable and aged platitude, but would like to modify it by this addition: Writing means trying to find out what the nature of things has to say about what you think you have to say. . . ."

"So the work of art is religious in nature, not because it beautifies an ugly world or pretends that a naughty world is a nice one—for these things especially art does not do—but because it shows of its own nature that things drawn within the sacred circle of its forms are transfigured, illuminated by an inward radiance which amounts to goodness because it amounts to Being itself." —Howard Nemerov,
"The Swaying Form: A Problem in Poetry"

"Poems, far from resting in nature as their end, use nature as a point from which they extrapolate darkly the nature of all things not visible or immediately knowable by the reason—to which visible nature is equivocally the reflexion and the mask. Such poetry is magical, then, because it treats the world as a signature, in which all things intimate to us by their sensible properties what and in what way we are."

—Howard Nemerov, "On Metaphor"

" 'Did I tell you my definition of a teacher?'
" 'No, I don't believe you did.'
" 'A teacher is a person who never says anything once.'
" 'Oh yes, I remember now, you told me that last week.' "

—Howard Nemerov, *The Oak and the Acorn* (1987)

"I set to work with three general principles to guide me—to be simple, to be sensible, and to be singable. I would still recommend them to any writer tackling his first libretto, but nowadays I would qualify them with certain reservations. Simple words can, and often do, sound feeble when magnified by music, as witness the lyrics of many musicals: something more than simplicity is needed. Sensible words, however apt dramatically, may be lacking in the intensity that music requires. To be singable is such a *sine qua non* of any text for music that I don't now know why I bothered to define it. The librettist must remember that he is at all times writing to be SUNG, not to be read from the printed page. His language must be the spontaneous expression of human feelings, and aim through the ear to the heart—unlike much contemporary written verse, which aims through the eye to the brain." —Eric Crozier, "The Writing of *Albert Herring*"
(*Opera Los Angeles*, IX.3, Spring 1992, page 5)

Goethe praised the *fürchtbare Realität*, the "frightful realism" in Horace's lyrics.

"And there's no such thing
as an insincere
erection is there?"
                —Thom Gunn, in his poem "Tenderloin"
                        (*The Man with Night Sweats*)

"The Body of / B Franklin Printer, / (Like the Cover
of an Old Book / Its Contents Torn Out / And Stript of
its Lettering & Gilding) / Lies Here, Food for Worms.
/ But the Work Shall Not Be Lost; / for It Will, (As He
Believ'd) Appear Once More, / In a New and More
Elegant Edition / Revised and Corrected, / By the
Author."   —Ben Franklin's epitaph, composed by
                Franklin when he was 22 (first version)

Asked if she had slept with General Eisenhower,
Marlene Dietrich replied: "How could I, darling? He
was never at the front."

Measure twice, cut once.

X is eating his seed corn.

"Schoenberg was a marvelous person. He gave his students little comfort. When we followed the rules in writing counterpoint, he would say, 'Why don't you take a little liberty?' And when we took liberties, he would say, 'Don't you know the rules?' "   —John Cage

∞

From Otto Preminger's *Laura*:
Dana Andrews: You know a lot about music?
Vincent Price: I don't know a lot about anything, but I know a little about practically everything.
Dana Andrews: Then why did you say they played Brahms's First and Beethoven's Ninth at the concert Friday night? They changed the program at the last minute and played nothing but Sibelius!

∞

"This fictional account of the day by day life of an English gamekeeper is still of considerable interest to outdoor-minded readers, as it contains many passages on pheasant-raising, the apprehending of poachers, ways to control vermin, and other chores and duties of the professional gamekeeper. Unfortunately, one is obliged to wade through many pages of extraneous material in order to discover and savor these sidelights on the management of a Midland shooting estate and in this reviewer's opinion this book cannot take the place of J. R. Miller's *Practical Gamekeeping*."   —Review of D. H. Lawrence's
Lady Chatterly's Lover, from the
November 1959 issue of *Field and Stream*

∞

At the Elizabeth Bishop conference in Key West, Octavio Paz remarked, summarizing Bishop's personality, that for her life was sad, but not serious. Beth Spires remembered that somewhere in her late notebooks, Bishop wrote that the three qualities she most admired in a poem were accuracy, spontaneity, and mystery.

"When I finish a film, I shake the tree hard and only keep what fruit stays on the branches."

—Cocteau to Chaplin

Not to *teach* a class, but to *conduct* it: I punch the tickets and call out the stops along the way.

Every revolution in poetry is inevitably followed by a reign of terror.

"I spent about half of my available time doing the chance operations and the other half writing letters to patrons. Both, I realized then, were part of the act of composing."

—John Cage

Henry James's nephew wrote in the guest book at Rye:
"There'll be no algebra in heaven
Nor learning dates and names;

But only playing golden harps
And reading Henry James."

"The soul is the prison of the body." —Michel Foucault

Denis de Rougemont: our central Romantic myth in Western culture is of a "passionate love at once shared and fought against, anxious for a happiness it rejects, and magnified in its own disaster—*unhappy mutual love*." (Tristan and Isolde) "What they need is not one another's presence, but one another's absence."

"I feed too much on the inward sources. I live too much with the dead."   —Casaubon

Freud's "law of ambivalence" holds that "loved ones are on the one hand an inner possession, an ingredient of the personal ego, but on the other hand are partly strangers, even enemies" (because of their dangerous exteriority).

"Put the best strawberry on the top of the basket. Cut. Cut. Cut."   —Lord Beaverbrook,
                                        to his newspaper writers

"The loss of contact with reality—there lies evil . . .
The remedy is to use the loss itself as an intermediary
for attaining reality. The presence of the dead one is
imaginary, but his absence is very real; it is hence-
forth his manner of appearing."   —Simone Weil

In a letter to Nikolai Medtner, Rachmaninoff explained that he let the coughing in the hall deter-
mine the length of his *Variations on a Theme of Corelli*:
"When the coughing increases, I leave out the next
variation. If there is no coughing, I play them in order. At one small-town concert, I forget where, they
coughed so, that I only played 10 variations out of 20.
The record so far is 18 variations, in New York."

Richard Taruskin, in an article in the *New York Times*,
recounted "an old and no doubt spurious tale about
Myra Hess, whose page-turner was mystified, during
an afternoon run-through, by the penciled mark-
ing 'L.U.' at various spots in the score where nothing
special seemed to happen. At the performance that
night, however, when the pianist came to the spots so
marked, she *looked up* heavenward."

Under the category of poetry-makes-nothing-happen,
it should be noted that between 1942 and 1944 the
BBC aired a nightly 15-minute broadcast in French,

narrated by Pierre Holmes and called *The French Speak to the French*. M. Holmes would often broadcast coded messages to the Resistance by this means. The D-Day invasion at Normandy on June 6, 1944, was signaled by a line from one of Paul Valéry's poems: "Long violin sobs rock my heart in monotonous languish."

Jean de Reszke's voice was described as having "le charme dans la force."

"My freedom will be so much the greater and more meaningful the more narrowly I limit my field of action and the more I surround myself with obstacles. Whatever diminishes constraint diminishes strength."   —Stravinsky

I received the following translation of "the mother of all rejection slips," which, according to *The Financial Times*, was issued by a "Chinese economic journal."

"We have read your manuscript with boundless delight. If we were to publish your paper, it would be impossible for us to publish any work of lower standard. And as it is unthinkable that in the next thousand years we shall see its equal, we are, to our regret, compelled to return your divine composition and to beg you a thousand times to overlook our short sight and timidity."   —Estelle Gilson, Bronx, New York

Silva rerum, a forest of things. Seventeenth-century term for a gathering of notes, occasional poems, copies of letters, memorable quotes, etc.

"Talent does whatever it wants to do: genius only what it *can* do." —Delacroix

Jean Cocteau: "Art produces ugly things that frequently become more beautiful with time. Fashion, on the other hand, produces beautiful things that always become ugly with time."

"A poem is always married to someone." —René Char

"Trust in God, but tie your camel." —Mohammed

"An original writer is not one who imitates nobody, but one whom nobody can imitate." —Chateaubriand

"Time goes by: reputation increases, ability declines."
                                        —Dag Hammarskjöld

Tolstoy said that boredom is the desire for desires.

When La Rochefoucauld wittily remarked that "we try to make virtues out of the faults we have no wish to correct," he might as well have been speaking of writers as they brood on their style.

"Deep learning doesn't shine."
                                        —Marie von Ebner-Eschenbach

"It is not so easy to make a name by an excellent work, as to make an indifferent work valued through a name already acquired."
                                        —La Bruyère

"Great minds discuss ideas; average minds discuss events; small minds discuss people."
                                        —Eleanor Roosevelt

"An uneasy conscience is a hair in the mouth."
                                        —Mark Twain

H. L. Mencken: "Criticism is prejudice made plausible."

"There are those who reach great depths only to release bubbles."
                                        —Stanislaw Lec

"Love and art do not embrace what is beautiful but what is made beautiful by this embrace." —Karl Kraus

"Celebrity: the advantage of being known by those who do not know you."
                                        —Chamfort

"The history of art is the history of revivals."
                                        —Samuel Butler

In her notes toward a book on Winning, photographer Diane Arbus took up the cliché "you can't win" and speculated that "when you do you have so much to lose." She cited the transience and anonymity of, say, Miss America or the Freckle King. "To put it a little gloomily," she concluded, "winning could be called the mark of Abel."

One of James Merrill's anagrams for MARCEL
PROUST was PEARL SCROTUM.

Give X enough string and he'll hang himself.

Balanchine said you choose music for dance not because you love it but because it makes you want to
move.

"A painting is the revelation of a discovery, not the
culmination of a plan."   —Picasso

"The nice thing about death is that I don't have to go
to any more poetry readings, and you do."
> —Joe Brainard, in the hospital towards the end,
> (reportedly) to a visiting friend

John Ashbery was visiting Yale (14 February 1995),
and attending a Silliman Master's tea. One student
asked the usual preposterous question: "What is

your relationship to the English language?" Ashbery paused, then stated: "Actually I write in the American language. The American language *includes* the English language."

∞

Tony Hecht telephoned this morning with an inadvertent parable. Decades ago, when he was living on Ischia, he knew a man named Daniel Bernstein—sad, unpleasant, and afflicted with Job's boils. Tony eventually made him over into the protagonist of "The Venetian Vespers." A week ago, Bernstein—a photographer, and long since living in San Francisco—telephoned to say that he and his wife would be in Washington on family business and might they dine chez Hecht. Since he is a strict vegetarian, elaborate and salady measures were taken by Helen to prepare a meal. They arrived—and left early. But the dinner, apparently, was excruciating. Bernstein turned out to be a boor—dull, querulous, annoying. Having the subject of one's poem to dinner—a subject that, in the poem, is vivid, sad, sympathetic, etc.—is usually disconcerting.

∞

"A man must not only be able to judge of words and style, but he must be a master of them too; he must perfectly understand his author's tongue, and absolutely command his own.   —Dryden

PORT IS LEFT, STARBOARD IS RIGHT!

A novice traveler once said, "How come I have a starboard cabin and a port hole?" A possible derivation of these two words goes back to the early days of ships. There was a certain kind of vessel which had a "steering board" suspended over the side of the ship and this acted as a kind of rudder. As most people are right-handed, the steering board was suspended over the right hand side of the vessel and so this side became known as "the steering board side" which was eventually abbreviated to STARBOARD SIDE. When these vessels came into the harbor it was safer to berth with the left hand side of the ship against the pier, thus avoiding any possibility of damaging the steering board. Hence the left hand side of the vessel became known as the PORT SIDE.

Payment of gratuities is a very personal thing. It is a reward for service given. "TIP" is derived from early British history, before the Postal Service, when stage coaches were the only transportation between London and other cities. Businessmen wishing to communicate with other businessmen would hand letters to stage coach drivers and offer a shilling "To Insure Promptness."

Graham Greene said that for a writer success "is always temporary, success is only a delayed failure. And it is incomplete."

"If we follow them of old time, we shall not follow
them."   —The Count, on the ancients,
                                    in Castiglione's *Il Cortegiano*

X is water under the burning bridge behind me.

X has written an unauthorized autobiography.

"To be able to say what a minor writer is—if it could be
done at all—would bring us a little nearer to defining
a culture. The tone of a culture cannot depend only
on the occasional genius, or the illusion of one; the
prevailing temper of a society is situated in its minor
voices, in their variegated chorus, but above all in the
certainty of their collective presence. There can be no
major work, in fact, without the screen, or ground,
of lesser artists against whom the major figure is illuminated."   —Cynthia Ozick

"What I see tires me and what I don't see worries me."
                                    —Mme de Sévigné, on sightseeing

"Her journalism, like a diamond, will sparkle more if

it is cut." —Raymond Mortimer, on Susan Sontag

La Rochefoucauld said that the wish to be exclusively wise is very foolish.

Virgil Thomson said that opera is all about saying good-bye while ballet is all about saying hello.

Pascal said that the last thing you get to know is what should come first.

Zeno the Stoic said that rhetoric is an open palm, but logic a closed fist.

"One line in the fourteen comes from the ceiling; the others have to be adjusted around it."
—Thornton Wilder,
quoting what he called one of the great sonneteers

Flaubert is said to have considered "the three finest

things God ever made are the sea, *Hamlet* and Mozart's *Don Giovanni*."

His old friend Robert Maynard Hutchins delivered the Commemorative Tribute at Thornton Wilder's memorial service in 1976, and quoted a letter he'd once received from Wilder about the effects of a bad review: "It's terrible to be humiliated that way. My barber lost his tongue and cut my hair in silence. The waitress at my *stammitsch* at Howard Johnson's murmured, 'Never mind, dear. Maybe you'll do better next time. You'll be wanting the eighty-five cent blue-plate lunch. It's hash today.' My dog hid behind the woodpile when I called him, and when I spoke to the little girl next door, her mother called through the window, 'Come inside, Marguerite, I think it's going to rain.'"

"Talent without genius is nothing much. Genius without talent is nothing at all."   —Valéry

"Nothing is more original, nothing truer to oneself, than to feed upon others' minds. Only be sure that you digest them. The lion consists of assimilated sheep."   —Valéry

"Laziness is the one divine fragment of a godlike existence left to man from paradise."   —Schlegel

"Except for music, everything is a lie."   —Cioran

"Poetry is made in bed like love."   —Breton

"The painter is always midway between design and anecdote, and his genius consists in uniting internal and external knowledge."   —Claude Lévi-Strauss

"One must paint a painting as one commits a crime."

"One doesn't make a crowd with fifty figures, one makes a crowd with five."   —Degas

The story goes that Barbra Streisand, at the start of her career, arrived at an important audition as a total unknown. She was chewing loudly a wad of gum. When it was her turn, she climbed onto the stool onstage, stuck the gum to the bottom of the stool, and sang her heart out, spectacularly. When she left, the casting director went up onstage and looked under the stool. There wasn't any gum.

Zeitoper—the term for the CNN opera of today.

"Oh, it will need some small changes here and there as we work," the Doctor said. "But it is a fine *schema*; coherent and simple for people who can't follow a difficult plot, but with plenty of meaning underneath. An opera has to have a foundation; something big, like unhappy love, or vengeance, or some point of honor. Because people are like that, you know. There they sit, all those stockbrokers and rich surgeons and insurance men, and they look so solemn and quiet as if nothing would rouse them. But underneath they are raging with unhappy love, or vengeance, or some point of honor or ambition—all connected with their personal lives. They go to *La Bohème* or *La Traviata* and they remember some early affair that might have been squalid if you weren't living it yourself; or they see *Rigoletto* and think how the chairman humiliated them at the last board meeting; or they see *Macbeth* and think how they would like to murder the chairman and get his job. Only they don't think it; very deep down they feel it, and boil it, and suffer it in the primitive underworld of their souls. You wouldn't get them to admit anything, not if you begged. Opera speaks to the heart as no other art does, because it is essentially simple." —Robertson Davies, on an opera in progress, from his novel *The Lyre of Orpheus*

"I feel strongly, and I think strongly; but I seldom feel without thinking, or think without feeling."

—Coleridge, in a letter

Willem de Kooning:

"The trouble with being poor is that it takes up all your time."

"In art, one idea is as good as another."

"I like a nice, juicy, greasy surface."

"I have to keep the paint wet so that I can change [the picture] over and over, I mean, do the same thing over and over."

"Flesh was the reason oil painting was invented."

"The goddesses—that grin they have. They really scare the pants off me."

"Don't be confused by surfaces; in the depths everything becomes law."   —Rilke

"Art does not reproduce the visible; rather, it makes visible."   —Klee

"Art is simply memory organized."   —Goethe

"Only those who are sad or else have been sad at some time need bother with my works." [Qui no és trist, de mas dictata no cut (e en algun temps que sia trist estat).]   —Ausiàs March, 15th-century Catalan poet

"Great writing is always a response to pain."—Brecht

"Death is what sanctions everything the storyteller can tell. Indeed, he borrows his authority from death."

"Only Zeus can rape the world with impunity. The rest of us must tell our parents what we've done."

"The great book of the future will consist of fragments torn from the body of other works; it is a reassembly, a patchwork quilt of meanings already accomplished. The great critic of the future will remain silent, gesturing firmly but himself unable, or unwilling, to speak."   —Walter Benjamin

"Why? I know that one horse can run faster than another. It makes no difference to me which one it is."
                              —The old Shah of Persia,
                          when urged to attend the Derby

Listening to Mozart is like looking at a time-lapse film
of flowers budding, opening, fading, a whole garden
of them. Listening to Brahms is a time-lapse film of
weather brewing, racing, darkening across a landscape.

"Deep calls to Deep, and Shallow to Shallow."
                                        —Emerson

St. Augustine, *Confessions*, from Book X:
But what when the memory itself loses any thing,
as falls out when we forget and seek that we may re-
collect? Where in the end do we search, but in the
memory itself? and there, if one thing be perchance
offered instead of another, we reject it, until what
we seek meets us; and when it doth, we say, "This
is it"; which we should not unless we recognised it,
nor recognise it unless we remembered it. Certainly
then we had forgotten it. Or, had not the whole escaped us, but by the part whereof we had hold, was
the lost part sought for; in that the memory felt that
it did not carry on together all which it was wont, and
maimed, as it were, by the curtailment of its ancient
habit, demanded the restoration of what it missed?
For instance, if we see or think of some one known to
us, and having forgotten his name, try to recover it;

whatever else occurs, connects itself not therewith; because it was not wont to be thought upon together with him, and therefore is rejected, until that present itself, whereon the knowledge reposes equably as its wonted object. And whence does that present itself, but out of the memory itself? For even when we recognise it, on being reminded by another, it is thence it comes. For we do not believe it as something new, but, upon recollection, allow what was named to be right. But were it utterly blotted out of the mind, we should not remember it, even when reminded. For we have not as yet utterly forgotten that, which we remember ourselves to have forgotten. What then we have utterly forgotten, though lost, we cannot even seek after.

How then do I seek Thee, O Lord? For when I seek Thee, my God, I seek a happy life. I will seek Thee, that my soul may live. For my body liveth by my soul; and my soul by Thee. How then do I seek a happy life, seeing I have it not, until I can say, where I ought to say it, "It is enough"? How seek I it? By remembrance, as though I had forgotten it, remembering that I had forgotten it? Or, desiring to learn it as a thing unknown, either never having known, or so forgotten it, as not even to remember that I had forgotten it? is not a happy life what all will, and no one altogether wills it not? where have they known it, that they so will it? where seen it, that they so love it? Truly we have it, how, I know not. Yea, there is another way, wherein when one hath it, then is he happy; and there are, who are blessed, in hope. These have it in a lower kind, than they who have it in very deed; yet are they better off than such as are happy neither in deed nor in hope. Yet even these, had they it not in some sort, would not so will to be happy, which that they do will, is most certain. They have known it then, I know not how, and so have it by some sort of knowledge, what, I know not, and am perplexed whether it be in the memory, which if it be, then we have been happy once; whether all severally, or in that man who first sinned, in whom also we all died, and from whom we are all born with misery, I now enquire not; but only, whether the happy life be in the memory? For neither should we love it, did we not know it. We hear the name, and we all confess that we desire the thing; for we are not delighted with the mere sound. For when a Greek hears it in Latin, he is not delighted, not knowing what is spoken; but we Latins are delighted, as would he too, if he heard it in Greek; because the thing itself is neither Greek nor Latin, which Greeks and Latins, and men of all other tongues, long for so earnestly. Known therefore it is to all, for they with one voice be asked, "would they be happy?" they would answer without doubt, "they would." And this could not be, unless the thing itself whereof it is the name were retained in their memory.

But is it so, as one remembers Carthage who hath seen it? No. For a happy life is not seen with the eye, because it is not a body. As we remember numbers then? No. For these, he that hath in his knowledge, seeks not further to attain unto; but a happy life we have in our knowledge, and therefore love it, and yet still desire to attain it, that we may be happy. As we remember eloquence then? No. For although upon hearing this name also, some call to mind the thing, who still are not yet eloquent, and many who desire to be so, whence it appears that it is in their knowledge; yet these have by their bodily senses observed others to be eloquent, and been delighted, and desire to be the like (though indeed they would not be delighted but for some inward knowledge thereof, nor wish to be the like, unless they were thus delighted); whereas a happy life, we do by no bodily sense experience in others. As then we remember joy? Perchance; for my joy I remember, even when sad, as a happy life, when unhappy; nor did I sense see, hear, smell, taste, or touch my joy; but I experienced it in my mind, when I rejoiced; and the knowledge of it clave to my memory, so that I can recall it with disgust sometimes, at others with longing, according to the nature of the things, wherein I remember myself to have joyed. For even from foul things have I been immersed in a sort of joy; which now recalling, I detest and execrate; otherwhiles in good and honest things, which I recall with longing, although perchance no longer present; and therefore with sadness I recall former joy.

"Bad artists always admire each other's work. They call it being large-minded and free from prejudice."
—Oscar Wilde

Magritte insisted, "We must think about objects at the very moment when all their meaning is abandoning them."

"Elegy is the form of poetry natural to the reflective mind."
—Coleridge

In Arabic the word for thirst can also mean voice, echo, corpse, brain, or owl. The word for dictionary also means ocean.

Morbidezza—"long, long melody," refinement of sensibility, an innate nobility of sentiment or utterance.

In painting, the advent of abstraction actually gave not just a new technique but more subject matter, by exploding (or at least disguising) the small established range of traditional motifs.

Formal poetry: rather like adoring the open sea, the clash of elemental forces, the overpowering scale of water and sky, the sheer majesty of sloops, the billow of sail and pull of line—and wanting both to study and pay homage to it all by building a model of a favorite boat—and then deciding to do it inside a bottle.

Edith Wharton, in *The Reef*, describes George Darrow as having "a mind in which the lights of irony played pleasantly through the shades of feeling."

"Memory has no power of invention. . . . It is powerless to devise anything else let alone anything better, than what we have already possessed."

—Proust, *The Fugitive*

"There are only differences."

—Ferdinand de Saussure

"This is not a novel to be tossed aside lightly. It should be thrown with great force."   —Dorothy Parker

"The difference between the *right* word and the *almost* right word is the difference between lightning and the lightning bug."   —Mark Twain

"If the cardinal virtue of poetry is love, the cardinal virtue of prose is justice."   —Arthur Clutton-Brock, in a piece included in *The Oxford Book of English Prose*

Thornton Wilder said a wastepaper basket is the writer's best friend.

Noël Coward described an Ibsen play as a play with a stuffed bird on the mantelpiece screaming, "I'm the title! I'm the title!"

"All deep things are Song."   —Thomas Carlyle

"There is nothing so absurd but some philosopher has said it."   —Cicero

"Our moods do not believe in each other." —Emerson

Robert Frost said that if your book has twenty-five poems, the book itself should be the twenty-sixth.

"Talent is long patience and originality an effort of will and of intense observation."   —Flaubert

In his pamphlet *Racine and Shakespeare*, Stendhal formulated the tone of his own works as "classical in style, romantic in ideas."

Moss Hart observed that, in the theater, stamina is as necessary an adjunct to success as talent itself.

∞

Oscar Hammerstein used to say that if the opening is right you can read them the phone book for forty-five minutes and they'll still enjoy the show.

∞

"Well, I'm polishing a little here and polishing a little there. The trouble is, the more you polish shit, the more it looks like shit."   —Burt Shevelove,
                when asked how the show was coming

∞

"It is the author's method to correct one work only in another."   —Victor Hugo, in the *Préface de Cromwell*

∞

Viennet, a 19th-century French poet, wrote a 30,000-line epic poem, which someone remarked would take 15,000 people to read.

∞

"I've never been to America, not to anywhere else, for that matter. Does that sound very snubbing? It isn't meant to. I suppose I'm pretty unadventurous by nature, partly that isn't the way I earn my living—reading and lecturing and taking classes and so on. I should hate it. And of course I'm so deaf now that I shouldn't dare. Someone would say, What about Ashbery, and I'd say, I'd prefer strawberry, that kind of thing. I suppose everyone has his own dream of America. A writer once said to me, If you ever go to America, go either to the East Coast or the West Coast: the rest is a desert full of bigots. That's what I think I'd like: where if you help a girl trim the Christmas tree you're regarded as engaged, and her brothers start oiling their shotguns if you don't call on the minister. A version of pastoral."   —Philip Larkin

"The immense appetite we have for biography comes from a deep-seated sense of equality."   —Baudelaire

Victor Hugo once described himself as "a cloud fettered by an iron chain."

"All great writers create two oeuvres, one deliberate, the other involuntary."   —Victor Hugo

"Accuracy is a duty and not a virtue."
                                                    —A. E. Housman

and that I do not like
writing in papers.

Papers have been known to
prosper without contributions from
me, so I daresay you will
not be too resentful to accept
my wishes for the success of
your scheme.

I am yours truly

A. E. Housman.

In old age, a public man, Hugo would receive guests daily, and tried to make himself as available as a coffee-table book: "Leaf through me."

Re *Leaves of Grass*, in addition to "leaves" referring to sheaves of paper, "grass" was a primitive term for compositions of little value.

Charles W. Eldredge told John Burroughs that Whitman had told him about the 1855 *Leaves of Grass* that it "was produced in a mood, or condition of mind, that he had never been able to resume, and that he had felt utterly incompetent to produce anything equal to it since. . . . That in contemplating it he felt in regard to his own agency in it like a somnambulist who is shown during his waking hours the giddy heights and impossible situations over which he had passed safely in his sleep."

"In matters of love it is easier to overcome a deep feeling than to renounce a habit." —Proust (and said by Auden to be his favorite French aphorism)

"Poets are the only people to whom love is not a cru-

cial but an indispensable experience, which entitles
them to mistake it for a universal one."

—Hannah Arendt

"What the American male really wants is two things:
he wants to be blown by a stranger while reading a
newspaper, he wants to be fucked by his buddy when
he's drunk. Everything else is society."

—W. H. Auden

"The chief sin is impatience. Through impatience
man lost Eden, and it is impatience that prevents him
from regaining it."   —Kafka

"A man should not strive to eliminate his complexes
but to get into accord with them: they are legitimately
what directs his conduct with the world."   —Freud

"There are no two things as important to us in life
and art as being threatened and being saved. What
are ideals of form for if we aren't going to be made to
fear for them? All our ingenuity is lavished on getting
into danger legitimately so that we may be genuinely
rescued."   —Robert Frost,
from a letter to Amy Bonner, June 1937

"Melodrama is the naturalism of the dream life."
—Eric Bentley

"Only the very greatest art invigorates without consoling."
—Iris Murdoch

"Of all the world's wonders, which is the most wonderful? That no man, though he sees others dying all around him, believes that he himself will die."
—*The Mahabarata*

Rabbi Pinchas said there are two kinds of death. One is as hard as passing a rope through the ring at the top of the mast; the other is as easy as drawing a hair from milk.

"One of the main reasons that it is so easy to march men off to war is that each of them feels sorry for the man next to him who will die."
—Ernest Becker

Santayana said that everything in nature is lyrical in its ideal essence, comic in its existence, and tragic in its fate.

Oscar Levant described Cole Porter as "a rich boy who made good,"

"I don't like that which resembles nothing."
                              —Igor Stravinsky, quoting
                              his own teacher, Rimsky-Korsakov

"Two elements are needed to form a truth—a fact and an abstraction."

"If the secret of being a bore is to tell all, the secret of pleasing is to say just enough to be—not understood, but divined."
                              —Remy de Gourmont

Jessie Benton Frémont, wife of John Charles Frémont the explorer, late in their life together, wrote of his fostering settlements in the West: "All your campfires have become cities."

John Cheever used to quote Cocteau: "Fiction is the force of meaning imperfectly understood."

"An author places himself uncalled before the tribunal of criticism and solicits fame at the hazard of disgrace. . . . If bad writers were to pass without reprehension what should restrain them?"

—Dr. Johnson, "Life of Pope"

Byron:

"Hatred is by far the longest pleasure;
Men love in haste, but they repent at leisure."

"Society is now one polished horde
Formed of two mighty tribes, the Bores and
    the Bored."

The Irish poet Austin Clarke, once asked by Robert Frost about his poetic method, replied: "I load myself with golden chains and try to escape."

"Absinthe makes the tart grow fonder."

—Ernest Dowson

Gide said of Stendhal that he was "the cuttlefish bone on which I sharpen my beak."

"A man may pretend to be serious; he cannot pretend to be witty."   —Sacha Guitry

"Whatever is not brought to consciousness will return as fate."   —Jung

When someone asked Claire Clairmont what she thought of Byron's morals, she replied, "It's the first I've heard of them."

"Buggers can't be choosers."
      —Maurice Bowra, when a colleague announced
                  his engagement to a plain woman

Sir Philip Sassoon once likened Lobster Newburg to a purée of white kid gloves.

Emerson's description of "double consciousness," wherein the "two lives, of the understanding and the soul, which we lead, really show very little relation to each other . . . one prevails now, all buzz and din; the other prevails then, all infinitude and paradise."

"Illusion is the first of all pleasures."　　—Voltaire

"This gave me some straw for the bricks of flattery."

"Nothing is too good for the proletariat."
　　　　　　—Marc Blitzstein, when asked why
　　　　　　he deployed his Schoenbergian technique
　　　　　　on music meant to inspirit union members

"In essence, the poet has one theme: his living body."
　　　　　　　　　　—George Seferis

English painter Pauline Boty, years ago, defined pop
art as a "nostalgia for now."

"No person ever looks miserable who feels he has the
right to make a demand on you."　　　—Goethe

"Every man is born as many men and dies as a single
one."　　　　　　　　—Martin Heidegger

"Against criticism we can neither protect nor defend ourselves; we must act in despite of it, and gradually it resigns itself to this."   —Goethe

"Hearing verse set to music is like looking at a painting through a stained glass window."   —Valéry

"So as not to be hurt before coming near the fire, he wraps himself in the metres."

—*The Taittiriya Samhita* (Vedas)

Mrs. Archibald MacLeish's favorite limerick:

> In the Garden of Eden, as Adam
> Was contentedly stroking his madam,
> He chuckled with mirth
> To know that on earth
> There were only two balls and he had 'em.

Anthony Powell:

"A good book demands a good index but a good index redeems even an indifferent book."

"A thief crucified between two Christs."

"Sonnets indicating the Young Man was a reviewer: LXXIV, LXXVII, LXXXII."

"Growing old feels like being increasingly penalized for a crime you haven't committed."

"Dogs have no uncles nor Kings relations." (Indian proverb)

"Life is a comedy for those who drink, and a tragedy for those who eat."

"Self-love is so often unrequited."

"Being Irish is like being homosexual, it gives the speaker a permanent topic of conversation."

"I really don't understand why people see the paintings of girls as Lolitas. My little model is absolutely untouchable to me. Some American journalist said he found my work pornographic. What does he mean? Everything now is pornographic. You see a young woman putting on some beauty product who looks like she's having an orgasm. I've never made anything pornographic. Except perhaps *The Guitar Lesson*."
—Balthus, in 1996

Alexander Woollcott is said to have remarked that

"reading Proust is like bathing in somebody else's dirty water."

"Without setting up any mystical dualism between 'the man' and 'the poet,' we have always to remember how far the creative artist is from being entirely absorbed and limited by the profane individual of biography. Goethe the privy counselor will never explain the whole of *Faust* . . . and Whitman the editor or government clerk is something less than the author of *Leaves of Grass*: the two are not mechanically identical. What the salaried citizen may think on the topmost layer of his mind is often, and familiarly, at war with what he may see or feel in his moments of deepest excitement and truest insight."
                    —Newton Arvin, from his study of Whitman

"Drawing is the probity of art."

"Drawing includes everything except the tint."
                                        —Ingres

Joseph Conrad's description of a man's life: "a rapid blinking stumble across a flick of sunshine."

Asked what his theory of education was, Robert Frost replied, "Hanging around until you catch on."

"None so poor that cannot swagger at a writing desk."
—H. G. Wells

In January 2015, two months after his death, there was a memorial service for Mark Strand at the American Academy of Arts and Letters. The speaker who told the best story was the playwright John Guare. He recalled that Mark had read a poem at the burial of Joseph Brodsky in Venice, and that after the service there was a reception at a palazzo. On a balcony, he found himself with Mark and Susan Sontag, who suddenly remembered once having seen a plaque on this very building commemorating the fact that Byron had lived here in 1818. She leaned over but could only see the top edge of something that *might* be a plaque. She wanted to lean out further and try to see the front of the thing. She asked Mark and John to hold her legs as she hung precariously over the balcony. The two men, each with an ankle in hand, looked up and smiled to one another at the sudden temptation.

"Fish have no word for water."
—an old Japanese proverb

"The pattern of the thing precedes the thing."

—Nabokov

". . . who speaks is not who writes, and who writes is not who is."

—Roland Barthes

"Witches are people who ought to like each other but do not."

—Philip Mayer

"We think that, as civilization advances, poetry almost necessarily declines."

—Thomas Macaulay, in an 1825 essay on Milton

". . . we want a poem to be beautiful, that is to say, a verbal earthly paradise, a timeless world of pure play, which gives us delight precisely because of its contrast to our historical existence with all its insoluble problems and inescapable suffering; at the same time we want a poem to be true, that is to say, to provide us with some kind of revelation about our life which will show us what life is really like and free us from self-enchantment and deception, and a poet cannot bring us any truth without introducing into his poetry the problematic, the painful, the disorderly, the ugly."

—W. H. Auden, in an essay on Frost

"If you're going to be a star, you have to behave like a
nun."   —Ethel Merman

"Oh, qu'ils sont pittoresques, les trains manqués."
[How picturesque do those trains later seem to us
that we failed to catch.]   —Jules Laforgue

"The law is reason without desire."   —Aristotle

In his essay on the sublime and the beautiful, Kant
found that men, Italians, and the night are sublime,
whereas women, the English, and the day are beautiful.

"This horrible duality has often given me matter for
reflection. Oh, this terrible second me, always seated
whilst the other is on foot, acting, living, suffering,
bestirring itself. This second me that I have never
been able to intoxicate, to make shed tears, or put to
sleep. And how it sees into things, and how it mocks."
                    —Alphonse Daudet, *Notes on Life*

Names of dogs in Shakespeare: Mocker, Mountain,
Silver, Tyrant, Blanche, Sweetheart, Crab.

"If you press me to say why I loved him, I feel that it can only be expressed by replying: 'Because it was him; because it was me!' "   —Montaigne

"Something unpleasant is coming when men are anxious to tell the truth."   —Benjamin Disraeli

"In its kind, which for me has no attraction, and in its metre, which for me has no beauty, I think it is a masterpiece."   —Gerard Manley Hopkins,
                    from a letter to Robert Bridges

"I sometimes look at the knot in a piece of wood until I am frightened at it."   —William Blake

"Thou has set my feet in a large room."   —Psalm 31.8

"And silence sounds no worse than cheers
After earth has stopped the ears."
          —A. E. Housman, "To an Athlete Dying Young"

"More pathetic situations and sentiments, that is, those which have a greater proportion of pain . . . may be endured in metrical composition . . . than in prose."
—Wordsworth

Alec Guinness, *A Commonplace Book* (2001):

"In Psalm 46 (King James version), the 46th word from the start is shake. The 46th word from the end is spear. In 1610, when the version was completed, Shakespeare was 46."

From the prologue of Edward Gordon Craig's book on Henry Irving: "We all have plenty of material to embroider on, whoever we come to write about, but one needs the nature of a malicious valet or soured lady's maid to dream of doing so—and some of their vindictiveness, to do the thing quite brilliantly."

William Hazlitt: "Cant is the voluntary overcharging or prolongation of a real sentiment; hypocrisy is the setting up a pretension to a feeling you never had and have no wish for."

Edith Wharton: "Every artist works, like the Gobelin weavers, on the wrong side of the tapestry, and if now and then he comes round to the right side, and catches what seems a happy glow of colour and a firm sweep of design, he must instantly retreat again."
(from *A Backward Glance*)

Anthony Trollope, on Dickens: "It has been the peculiarity and the marvel of his power that he invested his puppets with a charm that has enabled him to dispense with human nature."

Mark 8: 23–25:
"And he took the blind man by the hand, and led him out of the town; and when he had spit on his eyes, and put his hands upon him, he asked him if he saw ought.

"And he looked up, and said, I see men as *trees, walking.*

"After that he put his hands again upon his eyes, and made him look up: and he was restored, and saw every man clearly."

John Ruskin:
"It is not cheaper things
We want to possess,
But expensive things
That cost a lot less."

Frances Cornford, about Rupert Brooke:
"A young Apollo, golden-haired,
Stands dreaming on the verge of strife,
Magnificently unprepared
For the long littleness of life."

G. K. Chesterton, on Robert Browning: "It is original, not in the paltry sense of being new, but in the deeper sense of being old; it is original in the sense that it deals with origins."

Montaigne, *On Experience*: "For truth itself is not privileged to be used all the time and in all circumstances: noble though its employment is, it has its limits and boundaries."

Philip Larkin: "A love affair starts in misunderstanding, and ends in misery, with a lot of hysteria and introspection along the way."

"Have you ever seen a garden that will go into a man's sleeve, an orchard you can take on your lap, a speaker who can speak of the dead, and yet be the interpreter of the living? Where else will you find a companion who sleeps only when you are asleep and speaks only when you speak to him?"   —Al-Jahiz (c.776-868)

"I had to sink my yacht to make my guests go home."
                                        —F. Scott Fitzgerald

"Years ago I said to myself: 'There's no such thing as old age; there is only sorrow.' I have learned with the passing of time that this, though true, is not the whole truth. The other producer of old age is habit: the deathly process of doing the same thing in the same way at the same hour day after day, first from carelessness, then from inclination, at last from cowardice or inertia."

—Edith Wharton, A Backward Glance (1934)

William Dean Howells accompanied Edith Wharton to the first night of Clyde Fitch's dramatization of *The House of Mirth*. The play was not a success, not least because Wharton had insisted her heroine die at the end. Leaving the theater, Howells commented on this: "Yes—what the American public always wants is a tragedy with a happy ending."

Edith Wharton reports on Henry James's rapturous readings aloud of Whitman's poems. And conversing afterwards, James threw up his hands: "Oh, yes, a great genius! Only one cannot help deploring his too-extensive acquaintance with the foreign languages."

"If he but so much as cut his nails, one said at once that he was a greater man than any of them."

—Goethe, on Schiller

In *A Backward Glance*, Edith Wharton reports on Edward Robinson, a friend and director of the Metropolitan Museum of Art, who told her this story: "The young Heir Apparent of a Far Eastern Empire, who was making an official tour of the United States, was taken with his suite to the Metropolitan and shown about by Robinson and the Museum staff. For two mortal hours Robinson marched the little procession from one work of art to another, pausing before each to give the necessary explanations to the aide-de-camp (the only one of the visitors who spoke English), who transmitted them to his Imperial master. During the whole of the tour the latter's face remained as immobile as that of the Emperor Constantius entering Rome, in Gibbon's famous description. The Prince never asked a question, or glanced to right or left, and this slow and awful progress through the endless galleries was beginning to tell on Robinson's nerves when they halted before a fine piece of fifteenth century sculpture, a Piétà, or a Deposition, with a particularly moving figure of the dead Christ. Here His Imperial Highness opened his lips to ask, through his aide-de-camp, what the group represented, and Robinson hastened to explain: 'It is the figure of our dead God, after His enemies have crucified Him.' The Prince listened, stared, and then burst into loud and prolonged laughter. Peal after peal echoed uncannily through the startled galleries; then his features resumed their imperial rigidity and the melancholy procession moved on through new vistas of silence."

It was Shaw who said that when you learn something, your first feeling is that you've lost something.

In a newspaper article, director Nicholas Hytner: "It is a much quoted maxim that there are only seven stories. There are, apparently, Orpheus, Achilles, Cinderella, Tristan and Isolde, Circe, Romeo and Juliet, and Faust. All other stories are adaptations of those." And Lear?

When asked if she thought universities stifled writers, Eudora Welty replied, "Not enough of them."

Flannery O'Connor, in an interview, when asked about being a "formalist": "If you see, out of the corner of your inner eye, this shapely, delicate piece of pottery you want to create, and then you go to the store to get whatever materials you need, and you have an excess of them, but put your first allegiance to that palpable shape you have perceived—even if that means you will use hardly any of these materials—if that's your first allegiance, then I think you are a formalist. The alternative is to have the materials there, and to see what can be made of them, with first allegiance to those materials: you are willing to compromise on what I think of as the balanced relationship of all the parts. That balance is what 'form' seems to me."

※

"All power is of one kind, a sharing of the nature of the world."
                                                    —Emerson

⁁

"The port from which I set out was, I think, that of *the essential loneliness of my life*—and it seems to be the port also, in sooth to which my course again finally directs itself! The loneliness, (since I mention it!) what is it but the deepest things about one? Deeper about *me*, at any rate, than anything else: deeper than my 'genius,' deeper than my 'discipline,' deeper than my pride, deeper, above all, than the deep counter-mining of art."
            —Henry James, in a letter to Morton Fullerton

⁁

"Invention depends Altogether upon Execution or Organisation; as that is right or wrong, so is the Invention perfect or imperfect. Whoever is set to undermine the Execution of art is set to destroy Art."
                                                    —William Blake

※

W. S. Merwin writes of his having received, as a young man, a postcard from Ezra Pound, then in St. Elizabeths: "Read seeds not twigs. EP"

On his deathbed, Proust turned to Céleste Albaret: "Mon Dieu, Céleste, quel regret . . . quel regret!" [My God, Céleste, what regret . . . what regret!]

"The fine things we shall write if we have talent enough are within us, dimly, like the remembrance of a tune which charms us though we cannot recall its outline, or hum it, or even sketch its metrical form, say if there are pauses in it, or runs of rapid notes. Those who are haunted by their confused remembrance of truths they have never known are the men who are gifted. . . . Talent is like a kind of memory, which in the end enables them to call back this confused music, to hear it distinctly, to write it down, to reproduce it, to sing it."   —Proust

Once, towards the end of his life, Chet Baker joked with his fellow trumpeter Jack Sheldon about his drug-ravaged face. Baker said of himself that the lines were laugh lines. "Nothing in life is that funny," Sheldon replied.

Asked what he thought of Ivy Compton-Burnett's novels, the Cavafy translator John Mavrogordato said: "Greek tragedies acted by white mice."

"The proper, unique and perpetual object of thought is that which does not exist."   —Valéry

"In all great undertakings, tradition, in the true sense of the word, does not consist of doing again what others have done before, but in recapturing the spirit that went into what they did—and would have done differently in a different age."   —Valéry

Churchill told the story of the man who received a telegram announcing his mother-in-law had died and asking for instructions. The man wired back: "Embalm, cremate, bury at sea. Take no chances."

"What's important for the lucid ordering of a work is that all the Dionysian elements, which set the artist's imagination in motion and make the life-sap rise, must be subjugated before they intoxicate us; they must be made to submit to the law—Apollo demands it."   —Igor Stravinsky

"O gods: recognizing the beloved is god."
—Euripides, *Helen*

According to Roberto Calasso, in his *Literature and the Gods* (which footnotes *Archives épistolaires de Mari*, Paris, 1998), the first dream of which we have a record was told by Addu-duri, overseer of the palace of Mari in Mesopotamia, in a letter etched in clay tablets over 3,000 years ago: "In my dream I had gone into the temple of the goddess BZllit-ekallim; but the statue of BZllit-ekallim wasn't there! Nor were the statues of the other divinities that normally stand beside Her. Faced with this sight, I wept and wept."

"I like to write in mania, and revise in depression."
        —Robert Lowell, quoted by Jonathan Raban

Robert Frost, lecture-circuit veteran, said hell is a half-filled auditorium.

His wife Lizzie wrote in a letter about Melville: "Herman has taken to writing poetry. You need not tell anyone, for you know how such things get around."

Tonight I will make a list of my favorite books, while they are still vivid in my memory. I shall list them in no particular order, because there is no easy ordering of love. But first, a small list of exclusions. I will not include lapidary bits—poems or paragraphs that have enthralled me—because those stanzas of Leopardi or Yeats or Lowell would bloat things. I will not include books I once thought had changed my life—*Middlemarch*, say, or *Emma* or *Absalom, Absalom*—but, when re-read thirty years later, disappointed. There is nothing read during my childhood, when books like *The Sword in the Stone* and *Captains Courageous* instilled in me a passion for heroism and had as much to do with shaping my literary tastes as anything. The same for books read in college—works by Freud, Erich Fromm, Northrop Frye, Edmund Wilson. Though, the older I get, the more I want only to read non-fiction, I will exclude most of it here in favor of "literary" books, though I especially regret overlooking fine books on military history, and exemplary biographies—Walter Jackson Bates's Keats, Richard Holmes's Shelley, Richard Ellmann's Wilde, Leon Edel's Henry James, and David McCullough's John Adams. I shall also forego those *petits maîtres*—Colette, say, or E. M. Forster, or Sylvia Townsend-Warner—whose works I love but whose books have more savoir-faire than force.

Now to the favorites. *Leaves of Grass*; *Speak, Memory*; everything written by Tolstoy; *Madame Bovary*; the Psalms, Ecclesiastes and the gospel of Matthew; *In Search of Lost Time*; almost every story written by Alice Munro and Flannery O'Connor; the collected poems of Pope, Keats, Housman, Wallace Stevens, Auden, Larkin, Bishop, Hecht, and Merrill—with Auden as first among equals; *Lolita*; Sybille Bedford's *A Legacy*; *The Bridge of San Luis Rey*; the Rabbit trilogy by John

Updike; Edmund White's *A Boy's Own Story*; the major novels of Edith Wharton; *Great Expectations* and *Bleak House*; the *Iliad* and the *Aeneid*; Lorrie Moore's *Birds of America*; song lyrics by W. S. Gilbert, Cole Porter, Lorenz Hart, Oscar Hammerstein, Ira Gershwin, and Stephen Sondheim; many minor English Renaissance poets and major Restoration plays; Turgenev's *First Love*; Shirley Hazzard's *The Transit of Venus*; *As You Like It* (Shakespeare's tragedies and histories leave me unmoved but I invariably weep at the end of his comedies, in gratitude for their sublime, humane genius); *The Peloponnesian War*; *The Leopard*; Plato's *Symposium* and *Phaedrus*; James Merrill's *A Different Person*; *Nostromo*; the essays of Emerson, Wilde, Montaigne, and Dr. Johnson; *The Insect World of J. Henri Fabre*; both *A Hundred Years of Solitude* and *Love in the Time of Cholera*; Graham Greene's *The Honorary Consul*; *The Decline and Fall of the Roman Empire*; Eleanor Perenyi's *Green Thoughts*; Iris Murdoch's *The Black Prince*; Willa Cather's *My Antonia*; Toni Morrison's *Beloved*; the poems of Horace and Ovid; Elizabeth Bowen's *The Death of the Heart*; *The Red and the Black*; *The Tale of Genji*; Anthony Powell's *A Dance to the Music of Time*; *Don Quixote*; *The Pillow Book of Sei Shonagun*; Waugh's *Decline and Fall*, *A Handful of Dust*, and *Sword of Honor*; *The Sorrows of Young Werther*; the tales of Isak Dinesen; Cyril Connolly's *The Unquiet Grave*; *Democracy in America*; James McCourt's *Mawrdew Czgowchwz*; and of course the books by my husband.

But . . . damn! . . . why is it I am suddenly unable to recall the title of the one I like best of all . . . ?

"The great secret of morals is love; or a going out of our nature, and an identification of ourselves with the beautiful which exists in thought, action, or person, not our own."

—Shelley

"Even an author whose works were established, and whose works were popular, such an author as Thomson, whose *Seasons* was in every library, such an author as Fielding, whose *Pasquin* had had a greater run than any drama since *The Beggar's Opera*, was sometimes glad to obtain by pawning his best coat, the means of dining on tripe at a cookshop underground, where he could wipe his hands, after a greasy meal, on the back of a Newfoundland dog."

—Macaulay's description of "the writing game"
at the time of Dr. Johnson

"At least I know what I am trying to do, which is to live deliberately without roots. I would put it like this. America may break me completely, but the best of which one is capable is more likely to be drawn out of one here than anywhere else."

—W. H. Auden, in a letter to E. R. Dodds,
after having moved to America

"It is wonderful to be famous as long as you remain unknown."

—Degas

"Plot is for those who already know the world; narrative is for those who want to discover it."

—V. S. Naipaul

"My contact sheets may be compared to the way you drive a nail in a plank. First you give several light taps to build up a rhythm and align the nail with the wood. Then, much more quickly, and with as few strokes as possible, you hit the nail forcefully on the head and drive it in."

—Henri Cartier-Bresson

"Like more respectable pursuits such as scientific research and brokerage and practicing law, espionage is an organized search for windfalls."

—Charles McCarry, *Old Boys*

"I believe I could do it if it were in my nature to aim at this sort of excellence, or to be enamoured of the fame and immediate influence which would be its consequence and reward. But it is not in my nature."

—Coleridge, on genius

"Old age is respectable so long as it asserts itself, maintains its rights, is subservient to no one, and retains its sway to the last breath. I like a young man who has a touch of the old, and I like an old man who has a touch of the young."

—Cicero

"A mutual commerce makes poetry flourish; but then Poets like Merchants shou'd repay with something of their own what they take from others."

—Alexander Pope

"Against stupidity the gods themselves struggle in vain."

—Schiller

"Elegance is refusal."

—Diana Vreeland

"El diablo sabe más por viejo que por diablo." [The devil knows more from being old than from being the devil.]

—Spanish saying

"Only that which does not teach, does not cry out, does not persuade, does not condescend, does not explain, is irresistible."

"I have had to learn how hard is that purification from insincerity, vanity, malignance, arrogance, which is the discovery of style."

—Yeats

"A fact is what needs no meaning."

"Waking up confers on dreams a reputation they don't deserve." —Paul Valéry

"

"The function of art is to make that understood which in the form of argument would be incomprehensible." —Tolstoy

"

"I always worked until I had something done and I always stopped when I knew what was going to happen next. That way I could be sure of going on the next day." —Ernest Hemingway

"

"Style is the deference action pays to uncertainty. It is above all style through which power defers to reason." —J. Robert Oppenheimer

"

Gioacchino Rossini wrote that he had cried only three times in his life: when his mother died, when he heard Paganini play, and when a turkey stuffed with truffles slid overboard during a dinner cruise.

"

"The writer in meters, I insist, may feel as deeply as the non-metrical writer, and the choice whether or not to use meters is as likely to be dictated by literary fashion as by depth of feeling or sincerity. Nevertheless, they have become a conventional sign for at least the desire for some outward control; though their use cannot be interpreted as any guarantee of inner control. The very act of writing at all does usually imply an attempt to master the subject well enough to understand it, and the meters reinforce the impression that such an attempt is being made and perhaps succeeding."   —Donald Justice

"If all you have is a hammer, everything looks like a nail."   —Bernard Baruch

"In my youth I stressed freedom, and in my old age I stress order. I have made the great discovery that liberty is a product of order."   —Will Durant

"The glory of a library is an empty shelf."
                                    —Oliver Wendell Holmes

"Emma rediscovered in adultery all the tedium of marriage."   *—Madame Bovary*

"Aesthetics is to artists what ornithology is to birds."
—Barnett Newman

"Talent hits a target no one else can hit; genius hits a target no one else can see."   —Arthur Schopenhauer

When Edmund Wilson in 1940 suggested to Thornton Wilder that he write an opera libretto, Wilder replied: "After the age of forty, no. After the age of forty opera librettos are like driving a car: *Let George do it.*"

"They often spoil my breakfast but never my lunch."
—Gian Carlo Menotti, on critics of his work

"When people say opera isn't what it used to be, they're wrong. It is what it used to be, and that is the problem."   —Noël Coward

"I've learned from my mistakes, and I'm sure I can repeat them now exactly."   —Peter Cook

"Fame is a form of incomprehension, perhaps the worst."   —Jorge Luis Borges

The heroine in Edith Wharton's *The Reef* (1912) recalls: "In the well-regulated well-fed Summers world, the unusual was regarded as either immoral or ill-bred, and people with emotion were not visited."

"War is war, *l'art pour l'art*, in politics there's no room for compunction, business is business—all these signify the same thing, all these appertain to the same aggressive and radical spirit, informed by that uncanny, I might almost say that metaphysical, lack of consideration for consequences, that ruthless logic directed on the object and on the object alone, which looks neither to the right nor to the left; and this, all this, is the style of thinking that characterizes our age."   —Hermann Broch, *The Sleepwalkers*

"Is sex dirty? Only when it's done right."
                                                    —Woody Allen

"No snowflake in an avalanche ever feels responsible."   —Stanislaw Lec

Gabriel Fauré said he wrote his Requiem "for fun."

During the Great War, Hugo von Hofmannsthal—whose family barely had enough horsemeat to survive on—wrote a comedy.

Henry James's telephone number was Rye 51.

Louis XVI, the day the Revolution began, wrote in his diary: "Aujoud'hui rien" [Nothing today].

"Create like a god, command like a king, work like a slave."   —Brancusi

"Really, universally, relations stop nowhere, and the exquisite problem of the artist is eternally to draw, by a geometry of his own, the circle within which they shall happily appear to do so."   —Henry James

"The circle within which the Greeks led their metaphysical life was smaller than ours: that is why we cannot, as part of our life, place ourselves inside it. Or rather, the circle whose closed nature was the transcendental essence of their life has, for us, been broken; we cannot breathe in a closed world."

"Extremes? They meet in meter all the time.
   Any 2 realms can be made one by rhyme."
            —a notebook draft for "The Book of Ephraim"
                              by James Merrill

"What is Poetry?—The feeling of a former world and a
Future."   —Byron, *Journal*, January 28, 1821

Eckermann's diary, January 2, 1824: "We spoke about
the greatness of Shakespeare, and what an unlucky
position all English writers have, coming after that
poetic giant. 'A dramatic talent,' Goethe continued,
'if it were significant, could not help taking notice of
Shakespeare; indeed, it could not help studying him.
But to study him is to become aware that Shakespeare
has already exhausted the whole of human nature in
all directions and in all depths and heights, and that
for those who come after him, there remains nothing
more to do. And where would an earnest soul, capable
of appreciating genius, find the courage even to set
pen to paper, if he were aware of such unfathomable
and unreachable excellence already in existence? In
that respect I was certainly better off in my dear Ger-
many fifty years ago, I would very soon come to terms
with the literature already in existence. It would not
impose on me for long, and it could not much hold
me back.' "

Shakespeare, Sonnet 76:

"Why is my verse so barren of new pride,
So far from variation or quick change?"

cf.18, 59, 106, 130

The first appearance of the telephone in literature
was in 1878, in Gilbert and Sullivan's *H.M.S. Pinafore*.
In the octet, the Boatswain, Dick Deadeye, and Cous-
in Hebe sing:
"He'll hear no tone
Of the maiden he loves so well!
No telephone
Communicates with his cell!"
This was two years after the device was invented. And
"cell" no less!

"Thou comest when I had thee least in mind."
                                    —*Everyman*, about Death

10.v.08   The news is not yet public, but Knopf has
bought Nabokov's unfinished novel, *The Original of
Laura*. Chip has been asked to design it and was given
the manuscript; he brought it to S'ton for the weekend,
and I've just finished reading it. As a young man, when
I would wake up with a bad hangover, I always found

the best remedy—better than aspirin or sauna—was to sit in a darkened, cool movie theater and watch a brilliant film. VN's prose invariably had that same effect on me: everything else fell away, the mind took over from the body and clarified. The new, unfinished—or, to be frank, unstarted—material here reminds me that this effect was produced by sentences, one breathtaking one at a time. It happened all over again this morning: their weight and rhythm, their surprises and dash. And that Nabokov Effect is enough in itself. The book, alas, is nothing, a set of notecards clearly written by an old, sick man, preoccupied with his body and his past. Whatever is claimed was in his head, it is not on the cards. In its allusions and feints, yes, VN recalls earlier triumphs. And each of his sentences, even here, reminds me of an earlier surrender of myself to his sway.

⁂

Thomas Merton's description of the individual: "I have what you have not. I am what you are not. I have taken what you have failed to take and I have seized what you could never get. Therefore you suffer and I am happy, you are despised and I am praised, you die and I live; you are nothing and I am something, and I am all the more something because you are nothing. And thus I spend my life admiring the distance between you and me."

⁂

"Walk sober off before the sprightlier age
Comes tittering on, and shoves you from the stage."

—Alexander Pope

"In the world the self is what one least asks after, and the thing it is most dangerous of all to show signs of having. The biggest danger, that of losing oneself, can pass off in the world as quietly as if it were nothing; every other loss, an arm, a leg, five dollars, a wife, etc. is bound to be noticed."
—Kierkegaard, *The Sickness unto Death*

Paul Valéry: "God made everything out of nothing, and the nothingness shows through."

Carlyle: "The past is always attractive because it is drained of fear."

"The mere understanding, however useful and indispensable, is the meanest faculty in the human mind and the most to be distrusted: and yet the great majority trust to nothing else."
—Thomas De Quincey

The Lord's Prayer consists of 56 words, the Ten Commandments 287, the American Declaration of Independence 1328, the European Economic Community Directive on the Export of Duck Eggs 26,911.

Jules Renard: "Perhaps people with a very good memory cannot have general ideas."

"Just as 'La Bohème' does not leave much impression in the mind of listeners, it will not leave much impression on the history of our lyric theater."
> —Review in *La Stampa* of the 1896 premiere
> in Turin of Puccini's opera

"I have been buried along with my entire head."
> —Napoleon

In Rose George's book, *The Big Necessity: The Unmentionable World of Human Waste and Why It Matters*, a piece of advice devised by a Korean scientist, Park Jae Woo, is passed along: "Should the urge to defecate strike, take a pen, pencil, or blunt object and trace a line, deeply and with pressure, in a clockwise direction on the left palm or counterclockwise on the right. The urge, assures Dr. Park, 'will immediately cease.'"

Balzac described desire as a memory that hopes.

In the official Indonesian language, trains are called "snob-containers."

On his old TV show, Liberace would say, as if borrowing the words of a Greek god, "Why don't I slip out and get into something more spectacular?"

Tolstoy, *Anna Karenina*: "There was no solution but the universal solution that life gives to all questions, even the most complex and insoluble. That answer is: one must live in the needs of the day—that is, forget oneself."

I read in Moira Hodgson's new memoir about a couple who sublet Auden's St. Marks Place apartment one summer. Having navigated through the filth and clutter, the wife reverently lay on the great poet's bed the first night, and was suddenly, shyly curious to see what Auden kept in the drawer of his night table. She opened it. Inside were a pound jar of Vaseline and two pairs of castanets.

Charles de Gaulle remarked that "cemeteries are filled with irreplaceable men."

Among readers it is well-known that Hart Crane's father, a candy manufacturer, invented Life-Savers. It is less well known that Randall Jarrell's uncle, also a successful candymaker, created Goo Goo Clusters.

∞

"Anyone can be creative. It's rewriting other people that's a challenge."   —Brecht

∞

"A joke is an epitaph on the death of a feeling."
                    —Nietzsche

∞

"The ceaseless labor of your life is to build the house of death."   —Montaigne

∞

Dean Inge put it too bluntly when he said that all originality is undetected plagiarism. The more elegant and subtle formulation is Roberto Calasso's: "For every step, a footprint is already there."

∞

Henry James on Venice: "The deposed, the defeated, the disenchanted, the wounded, or even only the bored, have seemed to find there something that no other place could give."

In his book *Ardent Spirits*, Reynolds Price recounts a story told to him by Stephen Spender, in turn telling a story Leonard Woolf told to him . . . about his first outing with Miss Virginia Stephen: "They took a train trip to somewhere in the country, the day went well; but on the way home, in their private compartment aboard the train, Virginia was struck by a dreadful need to pee. It was one of the old carriages with no corridor, thus no hope of a loo. Of course Virginia didn't speak of her pain till she reached the point of cutting loose in her floor-length skirts. Only then could she burst out—'I'm dying, Leonard.' When he understood the cause, he took his copy of that day's *Times* and made a huge circular funnel with no open end. Appalled but overwhelmed, Virginia turned her face to the landscape, squatted above Leonard's improvised loo, lifted her skirts, drained her bladder, and threw the loaded funnel out the window. 'There was no way not to get married after that,' Leonard had said."

"I'll forgive and I'll forget, but I'll remember."
—Yiddish proverb

"Innocence is a leper without a bell spreading pain wherever it goes." —Graham Greene

"Of all the literary scenes
Saddest this sight to me:
The graves of little magazines
Who died to make verse free. "

—Keith Preston, 1920s

The archives of the Texas Department of Criminal Justice has, since 1982, noted the last words of those about to be executed by lethal injection for murder. Samples:

—Is the mike on?

—Man, there is a lot of people out there.

—I caused her so much pain and my family and stuff. I hurt for the fact that they are going to be hurting.

—Kick the tires and light the fire. I am going home.

—I said I was going to tell a joke. Death has set me free. That's the biggest joke.

—I love you, Irene.

—Tell everyone I got full on chicken and pork chops.

—Lord, I lift your name on high.

—Death row is full of isolated hearts and suppressed minds.

—The reason it took them so long is because they couldn't find a vein.

—You know I hate needles. . . . Tell the guys on Death Row that I'm not wearing a diaper.

—I deserve this.

—I'm ready, Warden.

—It's my hour. It's my hour.

From *The Guardian*'s obituary of James Lord, who died in 2009, this account of a problem and its solution: "He was expelled from one severe boarding school, but found Williston academy in Massachusetts little better. His writing ambitions were mocked by fellow pupils and when he told his father of his nascent homosexuality, Albert responded by arranging sessions with an analyst, who advised James to stop wearing Old Spice."

In *The Keats Circle*, edited by Hyder Edward Rollins, a comment by Richard Woodhouse about Keats is recorded: "He has said, that he has often not been aware of the beauty of some thought or expression until after he has composed & written it down—It has then struck him with astonishment—& seemed rather the production of another person than his own— He has often wondered how he came to hit upon it." In an 1817 letter to Haydon, Keats himself remarked "for things which [I] do half at Random are afterwards confirmed by my judgment in a dozen features of Propriety."

"Talent is a long patience."   —Buffon

"Leave them only their eyes to weep with."
—Bismarck, during the war of 1870

"On one occasion when the Buddha was preaching, the magic of his words became too much for him and he rose forty feet into the air, but he shouted down to the audience begging them to pay no attention; it would all be over in a moment, and wasn't of the smallest interest compared to what he was saying."
—William Empson, in his posthumous book *Argufying*

Henry James on the difference between a bad novel and a good one: "The bad is swept with all the daubed canvases and spoiled marble into some unvisited limbo, or infinite rubbish-yard beneath the back-windows of the world, and the good subsists and emits its light and stimulates our desire for perfection."

When he was asked, at age 93, why he still practiced the cello for three hours every day, Pablo Casals replied: "I'm beginning to notice some improvement."

"The structure of a play is always the story of how the birds came home to roost."
—Arthur Miller

"All great excellence in life or art, at its first recognition, brings with it a certain pain arising from the strongly felt inferiority of the spectator; only at a later period, when we take it into our own culture, and appropriate as much of it as our own capacities allow, do we learn to love and esteem it. Mediocrity, on the other hand, may often give us unqualified pleasure; it does not disturb one's self-satisfaction, but rather encourages us with the thought that we are as good as another... Properly speaking, we learn only from those books we cannot judge."   —Goethe

"The true work of a critic is not to make his hearer believe him, but agree with him."   —John Ruskin

"Grief is the agony of an instant: the indulgence of grief is the blunder of a life."   —Benjamin Disraeli

"We are born crying, live complaining, and die disappointed."   —Thomas Fuller

Tom Meehan told me of a friend of his who left at the end of a play saying "it was worse than I hoped."

Colette's last word, as she was dying: "*Regarde!*"

⸙

" . . . Accuracy is the basis of style . . . beauty walks along the edge of opposites, between pattern and freedom. If pattern is too strong, the play of fancy ceases, and beauty with it. . . . Style—to renounce all but the essential, so that the essential may speak."
                    —Freya Stark, *The Journey's Echo*

⸙

"The great task of life—sustaining culture—is to keep the invisible attached. . . . As the Greeks said of their gods: they ask for little, just that they not be forgotten."   —James Hillman, *The Soul's Code*

⸙

Gore Vidal once called Joyce Carol Oates "the three worst writers in America." Another wag called her "fecund-rate." (I disagree with both witty judgments, by the way.)

⸙

Suzanne Langer defined the comic experience as an image of "human vitality holding its own in the world amid the surprises of unplanned coincidence."

⸙

" 'Oh, certainly, "The Wings of Death" is not amus-ing,' ventured Mrs. Leveret, whose manner of putting forth an opinion was like that of an obliging salesman with a variety of other styles to submit if his first se-lection does not suit."

—from Edith Wharton's story, "Xingu"

∞

"If a disease has many treatments, it is incurable."

—Chekhov

∞

"Is it progress if a cannibal uses a knife and fork?"

—Stanislaw Lec

∞

"As far as helping me in the outside world, the con-vent taught me only that if you spit on a pencil eraser, it will erase ink."   —Dorothy Parker

∞

"If a traveller was informed that such a man [Lord John Russell] was leader of the House of Commons he may begin to comprehend how the Egyptians wor-shipped an Insect."   —Benjamin Disraeli

∞

"A poor, thin, spasmodic, hectic, shrill and pallid being."   —Thomas Carlyle, on Shelley

∞

"If you pick up a starving dog and make him prosperous, he will not bite you. That is the principal difference between a dog and a man."   —Mark Twain

Their styles are, of course, distinct, but in Anthony Hecht's "The Venetian Vespers," and in other of his poems set in Venice, you can hear the note struck by Ruskin about the city. Here, in the final volume of *Modern Painters* in 1860, with its cross-stitched Latinate nouns and sumptuous adjectives, are the tones of splendor and misery, gold and blood familiar from both writers: "A city of marble did I say? nay, rather a golden city, paved with emerald. For truly, every pinnacle and turret glanced or glowed, overlaid with gold, or bossed with jasper. Beneath, the unsullied sea drew in deep breathing, to and fro, its eddies of green wave. Deep-hearted, majestic, terrible as the sea,—the men of Venice moved in sway of power and war; pure as her pillars of alabaster, stood her mothers and maidens; from foot to brow, all noble, walked her knights; the low bronzed gleaming of sea-rusted armour shot angrily under their blood-red mantle-folds. Fearless, faithful, patient, impenetrable, implacable,—every word a fate—sat her senate. In hope and honour, lulled by flowing of wave around their isles of sacred sand, each with his name written and the cross graved at his side, lay his dead. A wonderful piece of world. Rather, itself a world."

Degas called Sargent "le chef de rayon de la peinture"—the department store manager of painting.

Octavian Maria Ehrenreich Bonaventura Fernand Hyacinth Rofrano.

Lanny Hammer, researching his James Merrill biography and leafing through Jimmy's Ouija board transcripts, found this entry about me, written in 1977: "JDM IN THE RIGHT DIRECTION NO CHILDERN + UNDIVIDED ATTENTION 2 WORK!"

"When one is young, one deifies and despises, without that art of nuance which is the finest gain in life, and understandably one must atone hard for having so battered people and things with Yes and No. Everything is arranged so that the very worst of tastes, the taste for the unconditional, should be cruelly duped and abused, until the subject learns to put a little art into his feelings, even to make a stab at the artificial: that is what the real artists of life do."
                              —Nietzsche, *Beyond Good and Evil*

In his novel *The Eighth Day*, Thornton Wilder defines a work of art as "power diminished to beauty."

CHOICE#! WITH

A SUMMER TAN. BUT. THEN... BI
LITTLE T.C COULDNT HE WAS T
ULL NAME (JDMc) 1943. P. JDM
AH. 1767 -1816. CATHOLIC MIS
M. MES CHGERS DO DO DO U WANT M

JDM IN the RIGHT DIRECTION
ATTENTION 2 WORK! NO. AS the
E DOWN ON A CROSS ?? (AC) NA
NOT AT ALL! WROTE 4 ESTATES L
NO 4. '13 TIN CORPORATED INTO C
AT 4. ALL HIS LAWS~
ALL THAT ENLIGHTEMENT MY I
T. (WHO DID NOT. DRESSED M
OF HONOR 2 MAINTENON! GRE
MS HE MUST WORK HE IS IN
ENLIGHtenment & IS NOW 2 BE S
. WE MUST NWRITE A ROMAN!
N LYRIC TONALITY + N MOMENT 4 SU

Asked during a BBC Radio 3 interview about Wagner's anti-Semitism, Georg Solti quickly replied: "If he can write music like that, he can kill me."

Wagner called opera "deeds of music brought to sight."

Goethe called translators "busy go-betweens praising as adorable a beauty only glimpsed through veils; they provoke an irresistible desire in us for the original."

Morris Dickstein quotes a wag who noted that a critic is someone who arrives late on the battlefield to kill off the survivors.

A line from Richard Barnfield's melancholy "Ode": "All thy friends lapped in lead."

David Hockney: "I'm quite convinced painting can't disappear because there's nothing to replace it. The photograph isn't good enough. It's not real enough."

Maupassant was said to eat lunch every day at the Eiffel Tower, the very sight of which he loathed. His lunch table was the only place in Paris he didn't have to see it.

Erwin Panofsky's definition of a portrait: "A portrait aims by definition at two essentials. . . . On the one hand it seeks to bring out whatever it is in which the sitter differs from the rest of humanity and would even differ from himself were he portrayed at a different moment or in a different situation; and this is what distinguishes a portrait from an 'idea' figure or 'type.' On the other hand it seeks to bring out whatever the sitter has in common with the rest of humanity and what remains in him regardless of place and time; and this is what distinguishes a portrait from a figure forming part of a genre painting or narrative."

David Hockney, on the double portrait: "There is always somebody who looks permanent and somebody who's kind of visiting."

Edith Wharton's description of one of her characters: "She wore the most expensive gowns with a penitential air, as though she were under a vow of wealth."

Brigitte Bardot: "It's sad to grow old but nice to ripen."

Proust notes that ardor is the only form of possession in which the possessor possesses nothing.

"One does not write, luminously, on a dark field; the alphabet of stars alone does that. . . . Man pursues black upon white."   — Mallarmé

Her niece Mimi told me that Dorothea Tanning's last words—on her deathbed at age 101—were "I'm on to the next question."

"Experience is never limited, and it is never complete; it is an immense sensibility, a kind of huge spider-web of the finest silken threads suspended in the chamber of consciousness, and catching every air-borne particle in its tissue."   —Henry James

"Solitude is not something you must hope for in the

future. Rather, it is a deepening of the present, and unless you look for it in the present you will never find it."   —Thomas Merton

A Chinese saying: "He who does not forgive digs two graves."

G. K. Chesterton's reaction on first seeing Times Square: "What a garden of earthly delights this would be if only one had the gift of not being able to read."

A 1926 telegram from Herman Mankiewicz in Hollywood to Ben Hecht in New York: "WILL YOU ACCEPT THREE HUNDRED PER WEEK FOR PARAMOUNT PICTURES? ALL EXPENSES PAID. THE THREE HUNDRED IS PEANUTS. MILLIONS ARE TO BE GRABBED OUT HERE AND YOUR ONLY COMPETITION IS IDIOTS. DON'T LET THIS GET AROUND."

Paul Valéry's definition of inspiration: "the act of drawing the chair up to the work table."

Vladimir Nabokov, on translation, in Chapter 7 of his

1947 novel *Bend Sinister*: "It was as if someone, having seen a certain oak tree (further called Individual T) growing in a certain land and casting its own unique shadow on the green and brown ground, had proceeded to erect in his garden a prodigiously intricate piece of machinery which in itself was as unlike that or any other tree as the translator's inspiration and language were unlike those of the original author, but which, by means of ingenious combinations of parts, light effects, breeze-engendering engines, would, when completed, cast a shadow exactly similar to that of Individual T—the same outline, changing in the same manner, with the same double and single spots of sun rippling in the same position, at the same hour of the day."

The Duc de la Rochefoucauld: "He who refuses praise asks to be praised twice."

Cicero, *De Amicitia*, "To be crushed by grief is the act not of a man who loves his [dead] friend, but of one who loves himself."

Kenneth Burke, to a class of undergraduates: "I don't intend to learn your names. You're all allegorical figures to me."

Frederick Raphael, in a review of a book about Hollywood stars: "Montesquieu accused the ancient Greek philosopher Xenophanes of implying that if triangles had gods, they would be triangular. A later wit remarked, 'Yes, but they would also have one more side than ordinary triangles.'" One sense of the divine is that extra, invisible side to anything.

Virgil Thomson, at a *vernissage*: "There're so many pictures you can't see the people."

Ned Rorem, in his diary: "An opera libretto cannot be multileveled psychiatry. It must be blood and picnics, hate and drinking-songs, love, ghosts, potions and posies. The music will give it subtlety."

Proust, in *Swann's Way*: "The past is hidden outside the realm, beyond the reach of intellect, in some material object (in the sensation which that material object will give us) of which we have no inkling. And it depends on chance whether or not we come upon this object before we ourselves must die."

Francis Picabia: "The greatest man is never more than an animal disguised as a god."

The drama critic Philip Hope-Wallace is supposed to have muttered while at the theater during an air raid in London, "How squalid to be killed at this disgusting little farce."

Benjamin Britten: "It is cruel, you know, that music should be so beautiful. It has the beauty of loneliness & of pain: of strength & freedom. The beauty of disappointment & never-satisfied love. The cruel beauty of nature, and everlasting beauty of monotony."

Auden, in his 1939 diary: "It is impossible to listen to music and get an erection at the same time."

Italian proverb: After the game, the King and the Pawn go into the same box.

Short of money late in her life, Ava Gardner remarked: "I either write the book or sell the jewels. And I'm kinda sentimental about the jewels." When the ghostwriter pressed her on certain details of Hollywood lowlife, she snapped: "Why can't we settle for what I *pretend* to remember?" But of her first husband, Mickey Rooney, she lamented: "It's a lonely business fucking someone you no longer love. Especially a husband."

A long-retired basketball player: "The older I get, the better I used to be."

John Updike, in a 2002 letter to Chip about the cover of a book, wrote: "Years ago—many years ago—I was struck by Raymond Loewy's (or somebody's) observation that a cigarette pack is such a successful package because it has the slight resilience of flesh."

George S. Kaufman as a drama critic: "I didn't like the play, but then I saw it under adverse circumstances—the curtain was up."

Cher: "The trouble with some women is that they get all excited about nothing—and then marry him."

Francis Bacon: "When I was younger, I needed extreme subject matter for my paintings. Then, as I got older, I realized I had all the subjects I needed in my own life."

Artist: What's your opinion of my painting?
Critic: It's worthless.
Artist: I know, but I'd like to hear it anyway.

"The wheel is turning, but the hamster is dead."

When attending the 2015 revival in St. Louis of an opera I wrote with composer Tobias Picker, *Emmeline*, which had premiered two decades earlier, I witnessed not just the opera (which, after so long, seemed to have been written by someone else) but the making of a genuine singing actress. The title role, originally sung by Patricia Racette, was undertaken now by Joyce El-Khoury, a young and very talented Lebanese-Canadian soprano. The final moments of the opera offer a black stage, a single spotlight on Emmeline as she sits in a chair and sings her last aria about why everything she has loved is gone. On the last note, the stage goes black, and the audience leaps to its feet with a thunderous ovation. The lights come up on Joyce, who takes a deep bow, and then walks slowly off-stage so that the entire cast can begin its bows. As she exits she wipes a tear from one eye, and then the other. The audience is cheering even more loudly. The cast takes its bow, and at the end the composer and I come on stage for a bow. As we back into the line for a few more general bows, I happened to end up holding Joyce's hand, and when the bows were over I kept holding it as we walked backstage. I kissed her hand and thanked her for a marvelous night. Then I whispered to her: "Those tears when you left the stage… Fake, I assume." She whispered back, "Of course." A born performer!

∞

Coleridge's translation of Plato: "In Wonder all philosophy began: in Wonder it ends…But the first Wonder is the Offspring of Ignorance; the last is the Parent of Adoration."

∞

Simone Weil: "Imaginary evil is romantic and varied; real evil is gloomy, monotonous, barren, boring."

∞

"For us, who have fared on, the silhouette of Error is sharp upon the past horizon."   —Max Beerbohm

John Updike: "The deaths of others carry us off bit by bit."

When they had both been in Hollywood for a while, composers Erich Wolfgang Korngold and Max Steiner are said to have encountered each other one day in the Warner Brothers commissary. "Tell me, Korngold," says Steiner, "we've each been working here for ten years already, and during that time your music has gotten worse and worse, while mine has gotten better and better. Why do you suppose that is?" "I'll tell you why that is, Steiner," Korngold replied. "It's because all the time, you are stealing from me—and I am stealing from you."

A literary curiosity. In Proust's *In Search of Lost Time*, Morel, the son of the narrator's Uncle Adophe, is a violinist and a rent-boy. In Tolstoy's *War and Peace*, Morel is an officer's orderly who, in a woman's coat, sings bawdy songs to his Russian captors. How could it be that a character with the same name turns up in the two greatest novels ever written?

"The Mesopotamians eventually started to want to write down things other than monotonous mathematical data. Between 3000 BC and 2500 BC more and more signs were added to the Sumerian system, gradually transforming it into a full script that we today call cuneiform. By 2500 BC, kings were using cuneiform to issue decrees, priests were using it to record oracles, and less exalted citizens were using it to write personal letters. At roughly the same time, Egyptians developed another full script known as hieroglyphics. Other full scripts were developed in China around 1200 BC and in Central America around 1000-500 BC.

"From these initial centres, full scripts spread far and wide, taking on various new forms and novel tasks. People began to write poetry, history books, romances, dramas, prophecies and cookbooks. Yet writing's most important task continued to be the storage of reams of mathematical data, and that task remained the prerogative of partial script. The Hebrew Bible, the Greek Iliad, the Hindu Mahabharata and the Buddhist Tipitaka all began as oral works. For many generations they were transmitted orally and would have lived on even had writing never been invented. But tax registries and complex bureaucracies were born together with partial script, and the two remain inexorably linked to this day like Siamese twins—think of the cryptic entries in computerized databases and spreadsheets." —Yuval Noah Harari, *Sapiens: A Brief History of Humankind*

Patrick Moynihan: "You're entitled to your own opinion but not to your own facts."

Robert Louis Stevenson: "There is no foreign land; it is the traveler who is foreign."

A phrase in Shelley's *Defense of Poetry* seems an exact description of how I write a poem: "imagining what is known."

On my bucket list there is only one item: learning how properly to die.

Sor Juana Inés de la Cruz: "ad impossibilia nemo tenetur" [no one is obliged to do the impossible].

Jonathan Swift, from his *Letter of Advice to a Young Poet*: "A commonplace book is what a provident poet cannot subsist without, for this proverbial reason, that 'great wits have short memories': and whereas, on the other hand, poets, being liars by profession, ought to have good memories; to reconcile these, a book of this sort, is in the nature of a supplemental memory, or a record of what occurs remarkable in every day's reading or conversation. There you enter not only your own original thoughts, (which, a hundred to one, are few and insignificant) but such of other men as you think fit to make your own, by entering them there."

Printed in the United States
by Baker & Taylor Publisher Services